God's Design

Making HIM Known

God's Battle
God's Design
God's Gospel
God's Names
God's Promise
God's Providence
God's Wisdom
God's Word

God's Design

BY SALLY MICHAEL
and GARY STEWARD

PUBLISHING
P.O. BOX 817 • PHILLIPSBURG • NEW JERSEY 08865-0817

ISBN: 978-1-62995-154-6 (pbk)
ISBN: 978-1-62995-155-3 (ePub)
ISBN: 978-1-62995-156-0 (Mobi)

Page design by Dawn Premako

Printed in the United States of America

Library of Congress Cataloging-in-Publication Data

Names: Michael, Sally, 1953- author.
Title: God's design / by Sally Michael and Gary Steward.
Description: Phillipsburg : P&R Publishing, 2016. | Series: Making Him known
Identifiers: LCCN 2015044420| ISBN 9781629951546 (pbk.) | ISBN 9781629951553
   (epub) | ISBN 9781629951560 (mobi)
Subjects: LCSH: Creation--Biblical teaching. | Women--Biblical teaching. |
   Men--Biblical teaching. | Christian education of children.
Classification: LCC BS680.C69 M53 2016 | DDC 231.7--dc23
LC record available at http://lccn.loc.gov/2015044420

Dedicated to John and Lorinda Donaldson,
examples of godly headship and joyful submission.

May God bless your ten children:
Jack, Caroline, Elizabeth, Wesley, Samuel,
Josephine, Abigail, Elijah, Simeon, and Benjamin.
May they be men of courage and faith who lead,
protect, and provide, and women of grace
and faith who nurture and help.

So God created man in his own image,
in the image of God he created him;
male and female he created them.

. . . And God saw everything that he had made,
and behold, it was very good.
—Genesis 1:27, 31

Contents

Preface

*Trust in the L*ORD *with all your heart,*
and do not lean on your own understanding.
In all your ways acknowledge him,
and he will make straight your paths.
—Proverbs 3:5–6

Gender confusion has increased exponentially in recent years, along with the normalization of homosexuality in the entertainment industry and the legalization of homosexual marriage. Now more than ever parents need to talk with their children in age-appropriate ways about God's good design for manhood and womanhood. Parents also need to talk with their children concerning how many ideas about manhood and womanhood—egalitarianism, feminism, homosexuality, gender blending/bending—go against the beautiful design of gender complementarity.

Children are encountering a confused and distorted message about gender at increasingly younger ages. Discussion of gender roles and identity can no longer be taken for granted or put off until adolescence. Children need to understand, before their teenage years, how God created men and women to be equal in personhood, dignity, and worth, and yet different regarding the roles He designed them to have. God's Word has a great deal to say about this and is more than sufficient to instruct us in this area.

Hopefully this book can serve as a springboard for further interaction between parents and children, not just about manhood and womanhood, but about God and the gospel. May the Lord bless you as you inoculate your children against the Devil's lies by speaking truth from God's Word, and may your children grow up to be godly men and women who spread the light of the gospel and live out God's design for men and women in a dark and needy world.

Introduction
How to Use This Book

This book was written to give parents an opportunity to present solid truth to their children and to encourage real-life application of that truth.

Relational

Children receive more encouragement to learn when truth is presented by a trusted individual. Your positive, relational parent-child commitment will be a real benefit when you sit down together to read this book. Your time together over the Word should be positive, affirming, and loving.

Interactive

There is a greater impact when an individual *discovers* truth instead of just hearing it presented. Many questions have been incorporated into the text of this book to encourage your child to wonder and think critically. The process of discovery will be circumvented if you don't give your child adequate time to think and respond. After asking a question, wait for a response. If your child has difficulty, ask the question in a different way or give a few hints.

Questions and responses can be springboards for more questions and discovery as you interact with your child's mind and heart. The Holy Spirit is the real teacher, so depend on Him to give both you and your child thoughts and truths to explore together, and to bring the necessary understanding. Take the time to work through each story at a leisurely pace—giving time for interaction and further dialogue. The goal should be to get the material into the child, not just to get the child through the material.

Understandable

These stories have been written with attention given to explaining difficult or potentially new concepts. Some of these concepts may take time for your child to digest. Allow your child to ponder new truths. Read the story more than once, allowing the truth to be better understood and integrated into your child's theological framework. At times, have your child read parts of the lesson, giving an opportunity for visual learning.

Because vocabulary can be child-specific, define the particular words foreign to your child. Retell difficult sections in familiar wording, and ask questions to be sure your child understands the truth being taught.

Theological

More than just acquainting your child with an understanding of biblical manhood and womanhood, this book is building a theological foundation for your child. As your child begins to correctly understand who God is and who man is, your child will begin to see the beauty of God's ways, the ugliness of sin, and the blessing of redemption.

Because the Word of God has convicting and converting power, Bible texts are quoted word for word in some parts. Some of these verses may be beyond the child's understanding, so you may want to explain unfamiliar words or thoughts. Even though clear comprehension may be difficult, the Holy Spirit often uses hearing the Word itself to encourage faith in your child (Romans 10:17). Do not minimize the effectual influence of God's Word in the tender souls of children.

Since the Word of God is living and active, allow the child to read the actual Bible verses as much as possible. Also, encourage your child to memorize some of the verses so he or she can meditate on them at other times.

Essential gospel truths are presented throughout the book. Use this as an opportunity to share God's work of grace in your life and to converse with your child about his or her spiritual condition. Be careful not to confuse spiritual interest with converting faith, and take care to avoid giving premature assurances. Fan the flames of gospel-inspired conviction and tenderness toward the sacrificial love of Jesus without prematurely encouraging your child to pray "the sinner's prayer."[1]

Application

Understanding the truth is essential, but understanding alone is insufficient. Truth must also be embraced in the heart and acted upon in daily life. Often children cannot make the connection between a biblical truth and real-life application, so you, the parent, must help bridge the gap.

Consider the following quotation by D. Martyn Lloyd-Jones:

> We must always put things in the right order, and it is Truth first. . . . The heart is always to be influenced through the understanding—the mind, then the heart, then the will. . . . But God forbid that anyone should think that it ends with the intellect. It starts there, but it goes on. It then moves the heart and finally the man yields his will. He obeys, not grudgingly or unwillingly, but with the whole heart. The Christian life is a glorious perfect life that takes up and captivates the entire personality.[2]

Spend a few days or even a week on each story. Reread the story, discuss the truths, and follow the suggestions in the Learning to Trust God section. Most importantly, help your child to see that God is who He says He is, and help him or her to act in response to the truth. Point out God's design in creation, and specifically in creating us male and female, and thank Him for His wisdom.

1. Some excellent resources for parents regarding the salvation of children can be found at www.childrendesiringgod.org, including a booklet titled *Helping Children to Understand the Gospel* and two seminars from the 2007 Children Desiring God conference, How Great a Salvation—"Leading Children to a Solid Faith" and "Presenting the Gospel to Children."

2. D. Martyn Lloyd-Jones, *Spiritual Depression* (Grand Rapids: William B. Eerdmans, 1965), 61–62.

Prayer

Ultimately, our efforts are effective only if the Holy Spirit breathes on our teaching and quickens it to the heart. Pray not only before going through the stories, but also in the succeeding days, that your child would see the beauty of God and His design and respond to Him in faith.

Knowing the Creator

If someone gave you a new game with a large board, different types of chips, spinners, dice, and colorful cards, would you know what to do with it? Would you automatically know how all the pieces work together and what each one's purpose is? Would you know how to play the game and enjoy it?

How would anyone know how to play the game? The only way is to first think about the game's designer or maker. After all, the game's maker is the one who designed it and made all the pieces work together in a certain way. Thankfully, game designers don't make us guess how their games are to be played. They give us instructions. By understanding the maker's design, you would know how all the pieces work together and you could start to enjoy the game.

The first verse of the Bible teaches us that we have a Designer, too—a Maker who has created us and designed us to work a certain way. The only way we can understand ourselves is by understanding the Designer and His design for who He has created us to be.

How can we figure out God's design for us? Thankfully, our Creator has not left us to figure out who we are and what we were made to do. He has given us His instructions in the Bible so that we can understand who we are and how we are meant to live.

In the Bible, God says we are created "in His image." Do you know what that means? That means we are created to be like God in a number of ways. By understanding who God is, we are able to understand ourselves, since He designed us to be like Him—"in His image."

Some people don't want to believe in God or follow His instructions for their lives. They believe they can know who they are and how they should live without following God's design. This is very sad. By not listening to God or receiving His instructions, they have no way of knowing the reason that God made them or how they were designed to live.

The Bible teaches that those who turn away from God and His truth become very confused. This is what Romans 1:21-25 says about them:

For although they knew God, they did not honor him as God or give thanks to him, but they became futile in their thinking, and their foolish hearts were darkened. Claiming to be wise, they became fools, and exchanged the glory of the immortal God for images resembling mortal man and birds and animals and creeping things. Therefore God gave them up in the lusts of their hearts to impurity, to the dishonoring of their bodies among themselves, because they exchanged the truth about God for a lie and worshiped and served the creature rather than the Creator, who is blessed forever! Amen.

Trust in the LORD with all your heart.

Proverbs 3:5

Those who do not honor, thank, and worship God end up confused about who they are and how they are to live. In order to understand ourselves correctly, we must first know God our Creator. We will never understand ourselves unless we start to know, honor, and give thanks to our Creator, for we were made to be like Him.

A great man once said that "man never achieves a clear knowledge of himself unless he has first looked upon God's face, and then [looks at] himself."[1] We must know and learn about God if we are to know ourselves and how we were designed to live. But how can we come to know God? How can we "look upon God's face"?

God gave us the Bible so that we can know what He is like and learn to love Him. God sent His Son, Jesus, to show us what God is like. When we begin to know and put our trust in Jesus, we begin to know God. When we put our trust in God's ways and in His instructions for our lives and say "yes" to Him, we come to understand God's good design for our lives.

If we try to understand ourselves and our lives without knowing God, we will only be confused and frustrated, for "in [Christ] are hidden all the treasures of wisdom and knowledge" (Colossians 2:3).

God has made you to know Him and His good design for your life. He has sent Jesus so you might be saved from the guilt, confusion, and power of sin. Will you say yes to Jesus? Will you put your trust in Him and welcome His design for your life?

Trust in the Lord with all your heart,
    and do not lean on your own understanding.
In all your ways acknowledge him,
    and he will make straight your paths. (Proverbs 3:5-6)

1. John Calvin, *Institutes*, I.I.2.

Trust in the LORD
with all your heart
Proverbs 3:5

LEARNING TO TRUST GOD

✦ Read Proverbs 3:5-6 again. Was there a time this week when you were tempted to depend on your own understanding, instead of trusting in the Lord and choosing His way? How can you acknowledge God in all your ways? What does this look like?

✦ What difference does knowing that you have a Creator make for living your life? How would your thinking and behaving be different if you didn't believe that you had a good and wise Creator?

✦ *Activity:* As a family, read and discuss Proverbs 12:15: "The way of the fool is right in his own eyes, but a wise man listens to advice." Discuss the two paths—the way of the unbelieving fool who is self-confident and does what is right in his own eyes, and the way of the wise believer who has entrusted his life and future to Christ. Make a poster showing these two ways.

We Are Not the Creator

The Bible says that God has made us in His image. That means that we are like Him in many ways. But does that mean that He has made us to be gods? Little gods, perhaps? No, we are not gods. We are creatures. He is the Creator, and we are His creatures.

This means that God is very different from us. How is God different from us?

God does not need anything, and nothing is too hard for Him. He is completely free to do whatever He wants to do, and He has complete power and control over all He has made. He knows and does all things perfectly and never makes mistakes.

But we are very different from God. We are just creatures. We need food and sleep and houses and other people. We can only be in one place at a time. We don't get to decide many of the things about our lives, and we are completely dependent on God for every breath that we take.

God says in the Bible, "I am the LORD, and there is no other, besides me there is no God" (Isaiah 45:5). God is the only God there is, and we are not gods. No one has the kind of power or understanding that He has.

God decided when and where you would be born and what family you would be part of. He decided what kind of hair you would have, what your skin and eye color would be, and whether you'd be short or tall. He decided whether you would be a boy or a girl. He made all these decisions for you, because He is the Creator and you are only a creature. He has charge over your life in a way that you do not.

God has decided many things about you that can't be changed. The Bible shows this when it asks, "Can the Ethiopian change his skin or the leopard his spots?" (Jeremiah 13:23). Of course not! No creature can change or should want to change the way God has made it. How foolish it would be if a leopard tried to change his spots or an elephant tried to change his trunk!

As creatures we must trust in the wisdom of God's design and embrace who He has created us to be. We must submit to and accept His choice and must welcome and be glad about His decision for our lives.

Have you ever drawn a picture of someone and then had the picture talk back to you and complain about how you drew it? The picture would have no right to complain or grumble against you. You designed it. You formed it. You made it.

In the same way, we should not grumble or complain to God about how we have been made. God designed us, made us, and gave us life. He has complete power and authority over us. We are just creatures, not gods.

This is what the apostle Paul says about those who grumble against God and His design for their lives:

But who are you, O man, to answer back to God? Will what is molded say to its molder, "Why have you made me like this?" Has the potter no right over the clay, to make out of the same lump one vessel for honorable use and another for dishonorable use? (Romans 9:20-21)

God has the right to make us and to do with us whatever He wants, because He is God. We have no right to complain or grumble against Him and His design for us. Instead of grumbling against our Creator, we should remember that we are creatures and should be thankful for the way He has made us.

The Bible tells us the story of Nebuchadnezzar, who for a little while forgot that God was in charge of his life. He forgot he was a creature and boasted, as if he were a powerful god, "Isn't this a great city I have built by my mighty power to show how great I am!" God was not pleased with this at all. To remind Nebuchadnezzar that he was a creature, God made him lose his mind, crawl on his hands and knees, and eat grass like an animal for a long time.

This punishment taught Nebuchadnezzar that God was in charge of his life. When his punishment was over, this is what Nebuchadnezzar said:

At the end of the days I, Nebuchadnezzar, lifted my eyes to heaven, and my reason returned to me, and I blessed the Most High, and praised and honored him who lives forever, for his dominion is an everlasting dominion, and his kingdom endures from generation to generation; all the inhabitants of the earth are accounted as nothing, and he does according to his will among the host of heaven and among the inhabitants of the earth; and none can stay his hand or say to him, "What have you done?" (Daniel 4:34-35)

We are all only creatures, and we should praise God for creating us and making us just the way He has. Let us say with David,

I praise you, for I am fearfully and wonderfully made.
Wonderful are your works;
     my soul knows it very well. (Psalm 139:14)

LEARNING TO TRUST GOD

✛ Read some of the questions that God asks Job in Job 38–40:2. What is the main point of God's questions to Job? What can we understand from these questions?

✛ How should being a creature affect our attitude about life? What difference should it make for us each day?

✛ *Activity:* With your family, list each of the "inalterable traits" (unchangeable things) that God has given you (e.g., eye color, hair color, skin color, height, build, family of origin, ethnicity, birthplace, birth date, native language, gender, and so on). Have you struggled to accept any of these? Why is this sometimes difficult for us? How should we respond to what our Creator has done? Draw a picture of yourself and label it "Designed this way by God."

Created Male and Female

Some people say there are only two kinds of living things on the earth: plants and animals. Do you agree?

What about man? Does man have leaves and roots like a plant? No, certainly not. Man is not a plant, that's for sure. But is man an animal? In some ways it may seem like man is an animal—we move around, eat, sleep, and raise our babies. Like many animals, we have eyes, ears, noses, mouths, hair, teeth, and toes.

But is man really an animal? No. The Bible says he is not. Of all God's creatures, man is something special and unique—there is no other creature like man. The Bible says that, on the same day God made the animals that walk, creep, and crawl upon the earth, He also created man. But He created man special. God said,

> Let us make man in our image, after our likeness. And let them have dominion over the fish of the sea and over the birds of the heavens and over the livestock and over all the earth and over every creeping thing that creeps on the earth. (Genesis 1:26)

So God created man special—He created man in His image and after His likeness. This means that He made us a little bit like Him. We were created to show the other creatures a little bit of what God is like. God has also put us in charge over all the animals. This is what the Bible means when it says that we have "dominion" over the animals.

God's desire is that we, His most special creation, would all together have lots and lots of children so that the whole earth might be filled with creatures made in His image. This is what the Bible says:

So God created man in his own image, in the image of God he created him; male and female he created them. And God blessed them. And God said to them, "Be fruitful and multiply and fill the earth and subdue it, and have dominion over the fish of the sea and over the birds of the heavens and over every living thing that moves on the earth." (Genesis 1:27-28)

God created man as male and female so that we could fill the earth with people. He created boys and girls who would grow up into men and women so that some of them might become mommies and daddies and fill the earth with more and more children, according to His good design.

It is a wonderful thing that God has created us as male and female. It would not be good if there were only men in the world, and it would not be good if there were only women in the world. God knew that it was not good for Adam to be alone in the garden[1] and, instead of creating another man, God created Eve, a woman.

God created both men and women and made them very different—not just with different kinds of bodies, but with different ways of thinking, feeling, acting, and relating to others. Have you noticed some of the many ways that boys and girls are different? Girls usually like dolls and tea sets more than boys do, and boys usually like trucks and toy guns more than girls do. There are many ways that girls are different from boys, and these differences are created by God. Can you think of some of these ways?

God made boys and girls to be different on purpose. But not everyone thinks that the differences between men and women are good or that God's design of making us male and female is a good thing. Some people do not think that boys should grow up to be manly (or "masculine") or that girls should grow up to be womanly (or "feminine"). Some think men should act like women, and women should act like men, and that all should dress alike, act alike, and do everything the same way.

But God has not designed us this way. God has designed us with real differences. A boy will never be able to become a mommy, and a girl will never be able to become a daddy. We cannot change this. Boys are designed to become men, and girls are designed to become women. We cannot change the way God has made us. God has made us either male or female, and this is a good thing.

1. See Genesis 2:18.

If you are a girl, are you thankful that you are a girl? You should be. God has made this a big part of who you are, and you should celebrate all that it means to be a girl. If you are a boy, God has made you a boy. Are you thankful that you are a boy? You should be.

Each of us should thank God for making us as male or female. It is part of His good design for us, and He knows what is best for our lives!

LEARNING TO TRUST GOD

✛ Read Genesis 1:24–31. How is man like the animals, and how is he different? Why is human life more important than animal life? What does it mean to have "dominion" over the animals? How does man show his dominion over animals?

✛ Girls, have you accepted and embraced the fact that God made you a girl and not a boy? Boys, have you accepted and embraced the fact that God made you a boy and not a girl? Take a moment to thank God for making you who you are!

✛ *Activity:* Discuss with your parents the ways that men and women behave differently. With their help, make a list of differences between men and women. Then go with your parents to a mall and notice how men and women are showing or not showing God's good design.

God's Design for Man

Do you know the names of the first man and the first woman? Their names were Adam and Eve. God created them in the garden of Eden long ago. They were the first people ever, and the Bible tells us how He created them both. The way in which God made them teaches us some very important lessons about God's design for both men and women today.

God created Adam in a way that teaches all men about what it means to be created as a man. God also created Eve in a way that teaches all women what it means to be a woman. In creating Adam and Eve, God made them to be a pattern or a model for all men and women to follow. Just as a toy car is patterned after—or made like—a real car, or a dollhouse is patterned after a real house, all men are patterned after Adam, and all women are patterned after Eve.

Let's read how God made Adam, the first man, and Eve, the first woman. The Bible says,

The LORD God formed the man of dust from the ground and breathed into his nostrils the breath of life, and the man became a living creature. . . . The LORD God took the man and put him in the garden of Eden to work it and keep it. And the LORD God commanded the man, saying, "You may surely eat of every tree of the garden, but of the tree of the knowledge of good and evil you shall not eat, for in the day that you eat of it you shall surely die." Then the LORD God said, "It is not good that the man should be alone; I will make him a helper fit for him." Now out of the ground the LORD God had formed every beast of the field and every bird of the heavens and brought them to the man to see what he would call them. And whatever the man called every living creature, that was its name. The man gave names to all livestock and to the birds of the heavens and to every beast of the field. But for Adam there was not found a helper fit for him. So the LORD God caused a deep sleep to fall upon the man, and while he slept took one of his ribs and closed up its place with flesh. And the rib that the LORD God had taken from the man he made into a woman and brought her to the man. Then the man said, "This at last is bone of my bones and flesh of my flesh; she shall be called Woman, because she was taken out of Man." (Genesis 2:7, 15–23)

We read in the Bible that God created Adam first. By doing this, God made Adam, the man, the *head* over the woman. Do you know what this means? The word *head* or *headship* means that God created the first man to be in a special

position or place of authority and responsibility over the woman. He was to be in charge of her and to take care of her. This was the special job that God gave man to do. Even though God created the man and the woman both as His special creatures, and even though both were created just as much in His image, God gave the man a special job to do.

Not everyone can have the same job. Not every soldier can be the captain of the army, and not everyone who gets on an airplane can be the pilot. God gives different jobs to different people. So even though we are all equal in importance and are made in God's image, some people have different jobs than others have.

Adam's job was to be the head over the woman. He was to be her leader, her provider, and her protector. He had special responsibility to take care of her. This was a special and important job for him to do!

Did you notice in the Bible that God made Adam first? God gave him the name *Adam*, which means "man," and God gave to Adam the work that He wanted man to do. He also gave Adam the command not to eat of the one tree. Adam was especially responsible for making sure that this command was kept.

God also gave Adam the job of naming all the creatures He had made. When you get to name something, you have a kind of "headship" or authority over it—you are in charge of it. Who gave you your name? Did your parents name you? They named you because they are in charge of you and are responsible for you. That is why Adam got to name Eve, and he called her *woman*, which means "from man."

All these things teach us that God gave man a special role of headship. Men have the special job of being a leader, provider, and protector.

What changes about a woman's name when she gets married? When a woman gets married, she usually stops using her old last name and takes the last name of her husband. When she was born, she was under her father's headship and shared his last name. But when she gets married, she usually takes on her husband's last name to show her husband's headship over her and her family. She does this because he, the man, is in a special position as "head"—as one who has a special job of being the leader, provider, and protector. This is the job that God has designed for men.

Adam's headship over Eve in the garden sets the pattern or design for male headship in our lives today. Paul followed this pattern in his teaching to Timothy when he wrote, "I do not permit a woman to teach or to exercise authority over a man; rather, she is to remain quiet. For Adam was formed first, then Eve" (1 Timothy 2:12–13). He also wrote, "I want you to understand that the head of every man is Christ, the head of a wife is her husband, and the head of Christ is God" (1 Corinthians 11:3).

The headship of Adam over Eve from the very beginning teaches us part of God's good design for men and women today. In order to understand what it means to be a man or a woman today, we need to understand how the first man and woman were created and designed to live in the garden of Eden together, before there was any sin and when everything was "very good" (Genesis 1:31). Are you ready to accept this good design for your life?

LEARNING TO TRUST GOD

✤ Read Genesis 2:5–23. Who was created first? Who does God give His commands to? Who names both the animals and also the first woman? What does Adam's name mean, and what does the word *woman* mean?

✤ After the fall of man, who does God address? (See Genesis 3:9.) Why does God speak to Adam first? Even though Eve sinned first, who is seen by God as the head of the human race? (See 1 Corinthians 15:22.)

✤ *Activity:* Make a list of situations in which there can only be one leader. What problems would there be if two people tried to be the leader? Play a game of "Follow the Leader" with two leaders. Does it work?

God's Design for Woman

Have you ever been stuck in a bad situation and needed help getting out of it? Or maybe you've gotten stuck on a math problem and needed help to finish it. All of us get stuck and need help every now and then, and how good it is that God has given us helpers! Helpers are wonderful gifts of God to us all.

Of course, the best helper of all is God Himself. David said in the Bible, "Behold, God is my helper" (Psalm 54:4) and "The LORD is on my side as my helper" (Psalm 118:7). God helps those who call on Him, and He also provides good helpers for us.

Before God made Eve, Adam was all alone. When Adam was by himself in the garden, God knew that it was not good. He knew that Adam needed a helper. Before God made the woman, He said, "It is not good that the man [Adam] should be alone; I will make him a helper fit for him" (Genesis 2:18). And from Adam's own flesh, God formed a woman for Adam to be his companion and his helper. This is why woman was created, and this is the way she was designed. The Bible says that the woman was made "from [the] man" and "for [the] man" (1 Corinthians 11:8–9).

Adam had been given work to do, and none of the animals could give Adam the kind of help that he needed. From among the animals, there may have been an elephant or an ox that could have helped Adam lift or carry something, but none of them could give Adam just the right kind of help and companionship that a woman could. Man needed more than a strong animal to lift, pull, or carry something. The animals could not fully share in Adam's work by giving him thoughtful suggestions, helpful ideas, friendship, and encouragement in the way that a woman could. Neither could the animals help Adam to obey the command to multiply and fill the earth. If Adam was to "be fruitful and multiply" (Genesis 1:22) and have children as God had told him to, who would be the mother? Adam needed help with the work that God wanted him to do, and only the woman could help him do it. She was the perfect partner to the man in every way.

Do you know what the word *complement* means? To *complement* something is to make it complete, and that's what Eve did. She made Adam complete. Man was incomplete in the garden without the woman. Adam needed her to be his helper and his companion.

Adam had been given the job of headship—of leading, providing, and protecting—and so Eve was given the job of helping, supporting, and submitting to (or accepting) his leadership. He was designed to be her "head," while she was designed to be under his headship (1 Corinthians 11:3). Even though Adam and Eve were equal and made out of the same "stuff," Adam was given a special job of leadership, and Eve was given the special job of helping by supporting him, submitting to him, and following his lead.

Eve, as the first woman, was designed to complement—or complete—the first man in his design. All women who have come after her have been designed in the same way. Women have been specially designed by God to do the work of helping, supporting, and submitting to the man that God has put over them as their head.

God knows that for any two people to work closely together as a team, it works best if one is the leader and one is the helper. If two people try to be the leader at the same time, what happens when they disagree? They would fight and not work together very well. God was wise and good to make man the leader and woman the helper. When the husband leads and the wife helps, the two complement each other. They are good partners!

Since the woman is designed to be a helper, does that mean that she is less important than the man? No, a helper is just as important a person as a leader is, and being a helper is something that God Himself does for us.

When God brought the woman He had just made to Adam, Adam was full of joy. He had just seen, thought about, and named all the creatures that God had made. And yet, when he saw the woman God had made, he was immediately filled with happiness, for God had made her as a perfect complement to him. Adam said,

This at last is bone of my bones
    and flesh of my flesh;
she shall be called Woman,
    because she was taken out of Man. (Genesis 2:23)

God has designed woman to be the perfect companion and helper for man. She completes him. Although God has given men and women different jobs to do, He has made men and women to complement each other and to find great joy in serving Him together. Isn't God's design good and wise?

LEARNING TO TRUST GOD

+ Read Genesis 2:18–23 again. How are men and women the same in this passage? How are they different?

+ What would a family, church, business, or nation look like if every person were in charge, and no one was a follower? Would it work for everyone in a family to be in charge at the same time? Would it work to have a company made up of only bosses, or a nation made up of only kings? Would this be a good design? Why not?

+ *Activity:* Make a list of some of the ways that your mom complements and helps your dad. Ask them for ideas and see what each of them says. Then work on a project together (clean out the garage, make a craft project, learn a new game, etc.) with Dad showing his role as leader and Mom showing her role as helper. How is this a good design?

Men and Women Are Equal

Which is more important: peanut butter or jelly? This is a silly question. Even though they are different, they are equally important for making a good peanut butter and jelly sandwich. Both are necessary, both are important, and both taste good!

Just as peanut butter and jelly are different and equally important for making a good sandwich, men and women are both different and equal too. Although they have different roles, men and women are equally important.

In the garden, God created the first man with the special job of headship, and the responsibility of leadership was given to him in a special way. The first woman was created for the man, to be his helper and companion or friend. So the first man and the first woman were given different jobs to do, but they were created equal—equally important, equally valuable, and equally made in God's image.

The Bible says that in the beginning,

God created man in his own image,
in the image of God he created him;
male and female he created them. (Genesis 1:27)

Man was designed by God as male and female. Both men and women are created specially in the image of God. Together they show the rest of the creatures a little of what God is like.

Being made male and female is part of what it means for us to be like God and to be created in His image. There are three persons in the one God—God the Father, God the Son, and God the Holy Spirit. This is called the Trinity. These three different persons are unified or joined together as one God, so God has both many-ness and one-ness. We have many-ness and one-ness too, since males and females are different and yet unified or joined together in the one human race.

Like the three persons of the Trinity, men and women are different from each other and have different jobs to do. Jesus, the Son of God, always obeys and submits to God the Father, even though the two are equal in power and glory. God the Father has a kind of headship over God the Son, but this doesn't mean that the Son is any less important than the Father; they are equal.

Just like in God the Father's relationship to the Son, the man has been given a kind of headship over the woman. We learn this from the Bible: "The head of every man is Christ, the head of a wife is her husband, and the head of Christ is God" (1 Corinthians 11:3). Even though their relationship and roles are different, a man and a woman are equal, and each is just as important as the other.

There are many ways that men and women are equal. Most importantly, they are equal in how God, our Maker, made us. Men and women are made by God from exactly the same "stuff." Do you remember how God made the first woman? God used Adam's rib to make the woman. So the woman was made from what Adam was made of. When Adam saw Eve, he said, "This at last is bone of my bones and flesh of my flesh" (Genesis 2:23). Adam knew she was not like any of the other creatures—she was his equal and his complement. She made him complete. Together, they were perfectly one.

Men and women need each other. It is part of God's design that men and women have to depend on each other. Women need men, and men need women. That is the way God made it to be.

> Woman was made from man, [and] so man is now born of woman.
> (1 Corinthians 11:12)

Men and women were designed to need and rely on each other for help in life and to do the work that God has given them to do. They are the same in how they need each other.

Men and women are also equal, or the same, in needing a Savior. Both men and women are equally sinful, so they both need God's grace in their lives. There is only one way for men and women to be saved from their sin. There is not one way for men and a different way for women. All who put their trust in Jesus are equally accepted and welcomed by God the Father. The Bible says that, for those who believe in Christ, "There is neither Jew nor Greek, there is neither slave nor free, there is no male and female, for you are all one in Christ Jesus" (Galatians 3:28). This verse does not mean there are no differences between the two, but that God equally accepts each person and equally saves each person who is trusting in Jesus.

Sometimes we might want to think that those who are different from us are not as good as we are. But the Bible is very clear that God designed men and women to be equal in importance and value. One is not better than the other. They are just different. God has given us different jobs to do. Men are to lead, and women are to welcome the headship of the man who God has placed over her and are to be his helper. But this does not mean that men are any better than women or that women are any better than men.

Instead of trying to be better than one another, we should all joyfully agree with God that men and women are equal, and we should honor and respect each other. Boys, how can you honor the women and girls in your life? Girls, how can you honor the men and boys in your life?

LEARNING TO TRUST GOD

✛ Read 1 Peter 3:7. In what way does Peter say that men and women are different? In what way does he point out that they are equal? Does having different strengths and weaknesses make one less important than the other?

✛ In many places around the world, women are not treated with the honor and respect they should have as creatures created in God's image. Why is this? How should we respond?

✛ *Activity:* Have your family list ways that each family member is different from the others. Who is better at what? How are you different? Take a moment to read your lists to each other and end by thanking God for how He made you different as individuals and yet equally important to Him.

Rebellion against God's Design

When God designed and made our world, it was all very good. There was no sickness, pain, sadness, or death. No person or thing was broken or out of place. There was a wonderful assortment of creatures, including zebras, eagles, dolphins, horses, cats, and squirrels. All the different creatures worked together perfectly according to God's good design, including the man and the woman.

God had created the man and given him the special job of responsibility, leadership, and authority (or headship). He had created the woman from the man's own flesh to be his companion and helper. God had made the man and woman equal but also different from each other, and He had given them different jobs to do.

God commanded Adam not to eat of the tree of the knowledge of good and evil. He gave this command to Adam even before Eve was created, so Adam was in charge of making sure that this command was kept.

One of God's angels, the Devil, turned away from God and became God's enemy. The Devil did not like God's beautiful creation. He did not like God's good design for the man and the woman. He hated God, and he did not like how the man and the woman were designed to show what God was like. So he set out to destroy what God had made.

The Devil came in the form of a serpent to get the man to rebel or turn against God and say no to His authority and commands. When Satan, the Devil, came to trick the man to sin, he did not come straight to the man. He came to the woman and tried to trick her. He told her lies. He told her she would not die if she ate the fruit. He told her she would be like God if she followed the desire of her heart to eat the forbidden fruit, which seemed beautiful and good to her.[1]

1. See Genesis 3:4–6.

When Eve took the fruit and ate it, she was saying no to the authority of God in her life. She believed that life would be better for her if she did whatever she wanted to do. She rejected the headship of God over her, and also the headship of her husband, by taking the lead and doing what her heart told her to do. She took the lead and led both herself and Adam into sin.

Where was Adam when Eve was being tempted to sin? The Bible says that he was "with her" when Eve took the fruit and ate it (Genesis 3:6). Why didn't he take responsibility for Eve? Why didn't he protect her from the lies of the Devil? Why did he stand by and let her be tempted and deceived and take the lead into sin? He too rebelled against God by not doing the job that God had given him of protecting and taking responsibility for the woman.

Both Adam and Eve said no to God's command, and both of them said no to God's design for them and to the jobs He had given them. Instead of following and helping Adam, Eve took the lead and led him into sin. Instead of leading and protecting Eve, Adam allowed her to be tempted and joined her in sin.

Do you know what happened after Adam and Eve sinned? They did what people often do—they felt ashamed and bad for what they had done and tried to hide from God. Here's what the Bible says:

> [After they had sinned,] they heard the sound of the LORD God walking in the garden in the cool of the day, and the man and his wife hid themselves from the presence of the LORD God among the trees in the garden. But the LORD God called to the man and said to him, "Where are you?" And he said, "I heard the sound of you in the garden, and I was afraid, because I was naked, and I hid myself." (Genesis 3:8–10)

When God asked Adam and Eve if they had sinned, they tried to blame someone else for what they had done. When God asked Adam, "Have you eaten from the tree of which I commanded you not to eat?" Adam tried to blame Eve and said, "The woman whom you gave to be with me, she gave me fruit of the tree, and I ate" (Genesis 3:11–12). In the same way, the woman tried to blame the serpent and said, "The serpent deceived me, and I ate" (Genesis 3:13).

The truth is, Adam and Eve had no one to blame but themselves. God had designed them to obey His commands and to follow His design for their lives.

God was in charge of them, and they were created to submit to His authority. Adam and Eve were made to follow God's design for their lives, but they were tricked into thinking that they could find a better way.

Instead of enjoying each other's differences, the first man and woman were now ashamed of themselves and began to blame each other. Instead of being happy, they were now unhappy. Sin spoiled God's wonderful creation.

LEARNING TO TRUST GOD

✛ Read Genesis 3:14–24. What were the consequences of Adam and Eve's sin? How did God cover the sins of Adam and Eve? Where do you suppose the "garments of skins" came from? How does this point forward to what God provides for us through Jesus?

✛ In what ways do you try to cover your sins? Do you make excuses or blame others? Do you ignore them and try not to think about them? How are these types of responses like the fig leaves of Genesis 3:7?

✛ *Activity:* How did your parents encourage you away from sin this week? Did you help others to walk *away from* or *toward* sin this week? Explain. Make a bookmark with the words to Psalm 119:11 on it. How can you store up God's Word? What is the difference between storing it in your head and storing it in your heart? Ask God to show you the beauty and goodness of His design. Pray for a heart that says yes to His ways, commands, and design.

Continuing Rebellion in Man

Have you noticed what happens when you drop a piece of fruit like an apple or a pear? When you drop a piece of fruit, it often bruises—it gets a brown spot on it. After it bruises, it gets soft and begins to spoil or gets rotten on the spot where it fell. Once fruit is bruised and begins to spoil, the spoiled part spreads and spreads until the whole piece of fruit is rotten and must be thrown out.

Just like a spoiled spot spreads on fruit, Adam and Eve's sin spread too. It spread to all that God had made. It spread even to the animals, which became wild and unruly and were now no longer free from disease and death. It spread to Adam and Eve's minds and desires and bodies. It spread to all their children, and it has even spread to you and me.

Adam and Eve's sin continues to affect our lives and our relationships with each other. After Adam and Eve sinned, God punished them by allowing them to experience the consequences of their foolish decision. Since they rejected God's design for their lives, He hardened their hearts so they would naturally continue to go against His design and experience the painful consequences of their choice.

This was what God said when He told Adam and Eve and the serpent about their punishment:

The LORD God said to the serpent, "Because you have done this, cursed are you above all livestock and above all beasts of the field; on your belly you shall go, and dust you shall eat all the days of your life. I will put enmity between you and the woman, and between your offspring and her off-spring; he shall bruise your head, and you shall bruise his heel." To the woman he said, "I will surely multiply your pain in childbearing; in pain you shall bring forth children. Your desire shall be for your husband, and he shall rule over you." And to Adam he said, "Because you have listened to the voice of your wife and have eaten of the tree of which I commanded you, 'You shall not eat of it,' cursed is the ground because of you; in pain you shall eat of it all the days of your life; thorns and thistles it shall bring forth for you; and you shall eat the plants of the field. By the sweat of your face you shall eat bread, till you return to the ground, for out of it you were taken; for you are dust, and to dust you shall return." (Genesis 3:14–19)

How was the serpent punished? The serpent would be punished by being defeated and destroyed in the end, by One who would be born of a woman and win the final victory. Eve and all the women after her would experience pain and difficulty in doing what she was designed to do. Women would now have pain

in giving birth to children, and their relationships with their husbands would be made difficult as well.

How was man punished? The man had been designed to be a responsible leader and faithful protector, but men would now experience frustration in their work. Their work would be very hard for them, and they would not want to do it. Instead of serving as faithful heads over their wives, men would not want to lead, protect, or provide as they should. They would let their wives take the lead and would just stand by like Adam had done, or they would try to "rule" over their wives with impatience and anger. Sin would have a kind of power over them so that they would not do what they were created to do.

Part of God's punishment for women was that "your desire shall be for your husband, and he shall rule over you." Husbands would now have sinful desires to "rule" over their wives, mistreating them with anger and impatience. Some husbands would "rule" over their wives with selfishness and laziness, and would even ignore their needs. Others would "rule" over their wives with harsh words, unkindness, and cruelty. This is not following God's good design, is it?

God had designed the man to be the head of the woman, and yet now this headship would be spoiled and changed from how God had designed it to be. It would be spoiled because of sin. Adam's failure or mistake in not being the man that God designed him to be would cause all men to fail to be what God had designed them to be—brave, hardworking, gentle leaders in the world.

Sin caused Adam and Eve great pain in their relationship with each other. There would now be fighting, arguing, and hurt feelings. Because of sin, men and women would continue to have pain in being together. Men and women now have sinful desires to keep sinning and going against God's good design.

But God did not give up on man and woman. He continued to show grace to Adam and Eve. He promised that another Son of Man would come to destroy the works of the Devil and to free them from the power of sin.[1] We all have a sin

1. See Genesis 3:15; Romans 6:22; 1 John 3:8.

problem that robs us from living in God's good design the way He made us to live. Only Jesus can wipe away our sins and give us the heart to love God's ways and God's good design.

> Therefore, just as sin came into the world through one man, and death through sin, and so death spread to all men. (Romans 5:12)

LEARNING TO TRUST GOD

✦ Read the story of Herod and his death in Acts 12:21–23. Herod was struck down by God (in part) because he "did not give God the glory" and did nothing when the crowd called him a god. Why is it sometimes wrong to do nothing? Think of other times when doing nothing (or "passivity") is a great sin.

✦ Besides passivity, what other type of sin can men fall into because of the power of sin now at work in our hearts? (See Genesis 3:16.) What does it mean for a husband to "rule" over a wife in a "domineering" way? How is this a distortion of God's good design for men and women?

✦ *Activity:* With your family, discuss the power of sin and sinful tendencies in our hearts. Ask your parents what sinful tendencies they have. Ask yourself what sinful tendencies you have. Is it okay to passively live with those sins? As a family, decide on something you can do to fight the sins of passivity, laziness, selfishness, and unkindness, and do something to bless someone else (rake leaves, make supper, wash a car, watch a dog, etc.).

Continuing Rebellion in Woman

Do you know what *rhyming* words are? They are words that end with the same sound, like *cat* and *hat*, or *cake* and *take*. Can you think of other words that rhyme?

This story is about what happened to women after the sin in the garden. You can remember this if you memorize these rhyming words: *pain, reign, disdain,* and *in vain*. Repeat these rhyming words and try to memorize them to remember this true story.

Do you remember how Adam and Eve rebelled against God's rule and design in the garden? Instead of obeying God and respecting His authority, they ate the fruit of the forbidden tree. Adam did not lead or protect his wife, and Eve was not a helper to Adam. Instead of helping Adam to do the right thing, Eve encouraged him to eat the fruit. Adam and Eve did not follow God's design for men and women or respect God's rule. They sinned by choosing their own way.

There is always a punishment for sin, and this was God's punishment for the woman:

> To the woman he said, "I will surely multiply your pain in childbearing; in pain you shall bring forth children. Your desire shall be for your husband, and he shall rule over you." (Genesis 3:16)

So the consequence of sin was *pain*—not only the spiritual and emotional pain of being separated from God, but for women the physical pain of giving birth to children. Ask your mother about the pain she had when you were born. It really, really hurt.

But that wasn't the only result of woman's sin. Instead of being happy about her husband's leadership and cooperating with him, women would want to be the leader. They would want to be in charge and control their husband. Women would want to rule, be in charge, or *reign*. This is not following God's design!

Have women stopped rebelling against God's rule and design? Very sadly, the answer is no. Some women even think it is good to change God's design, and they encourage other women to rebel against God's design.

Betty Friedan was one of those women. She wrote a book saying that women are unhappy because of men, and that their role as helper, wife, and mother makes them unhappy.[1] Is this what God says makes people unhappy? No, God says that sin makes people unhappy.

Betty Friedan and other women who wrongly think like her are called "feminists." They don't like God's design for men and women—they *disdain* it. Because they don't respect God's wisdom and design but *disdain* it, they encourage women to rebel against God's good design.

Feminists gathered groups of women together to spread the *disdain* or dislike of men and God's design. How did they do this? With their words. They started to complain. (Oh, another rhyming word!) They complained about men, about being at home, and about being wives and mothers. They complained about being led by men and not being in charge.[2]

1. Betty Friedan expressed her views in a book called *The Feminine Mystique* (New York: W. W. Norton, 1963), which was based on ideas expressed by French existential philosopher Simone de Beauvoir in *The Second Sex* (Paris: Gallimard, 1949).
2. "Feminists in New York discovered that if they gathered women together in small groups and got all those women talking about their hurts and grievances against men, then all the women in the group would begin to get upset with men, even those women who didn't have any hurts and grievances themselves, and then their anger could be directed into action" (Mary Kassian, "You've Come a Long Way, Baby!" [talk given at the 2008 True Woman Conference, Chicago, IL, October 10, 2008], available online at http://www.truewoman.com/?id=317).

What happens when people start complaining? Complaining spreads. Other people start complaining. Then more people complain. Soon lots of people are unhappy and complaining.

Women's rebellion against God's authority and design has caused much sadness in this world. Sometimes little unborn babies still inside their mother's bodies are killed in abortion because women want to be in charge of their bodies. Some women have blamed men for their problems and have left their husbands, not wanting to be married. Women have believed the lie that submission is a bad thing and have not wanted the protection and leadership of men.

All of woman's rebellion against God's design is *in vain*. That means that nothing good has come from it. God is still in charge. God's ways are still good and right. Sin is still wrong, and only unhappiness comes from rebelling against God's design for men and women. Rebellion is always *in vain*. It always causes suffering and sadness.

Sin causes *pain*. When women want to *reign* and *disdain* God's right to rule and God's ways, it is *in vain*. It only brings unhappiness to women and to others. Only God's design is right. Only God's ways bring happiness.

Ever since the fall, people have sinned and have wanted to follow their own way instead of God's way. We should never follow Satan's suggestions to rebel against God. We cannot make up our own design or follow the wrong thinking of the world. God's Word is true and tells us the way to real happiness.

Do not be conformed to this world, but be transformed by the renewal of your mind, that by testing you may discern what is the will of God, what is good and acceptable and perfect. (Romans 12:2)

LEARNING TO TRUST GOD

✢ Read Romans 12:2 again. What does "do not be conformed to this world" mean? What does "transformed" mean? What does it mean to renew your mind? How can we renew our minds? How can we tell what is right—what is the will of God?

✢ How does a father protect and lead his family? What kinds of things might a girl do to resist her father's authority? Why is this dangerous?

✢ *Activity:* As a family, take part in a prolife activity or do something to support prolife efforts.

God's Good Design Distorted

When a mother elephant and a father elephant join together, they make a baby elephant. But it would be very strange for a mother elephant and a father camel to join together. Actually, they can't—but if they could, what would they make? A camephant? An elemel? That would be a very strange animal. It would be distorted—twisted and all mixed up. But in God's design, elephants make baby elephants, and camels make baby camels, and they don't mix together.

God has a design for men and women too. A married man and his wife join together and make a baby person. God's design is very good, and from His design come beautiful babies—little boys and girls.

But just like men and women rebel against the job of leading or helping that God has designed for them to do, sometimes men and women or boys and girls rebel against what God has made them to be. God made a man to love a woman in a special way. But when a boy wants to love another boy in the way that a man and a woman love each other, or a girl wants to love a girl in a way that a woman loves a man, this is against God's design. This is called homosexuality, and it is a disobedience that brings much sadness and pain. It is against nature or the way God made us—just like a camel and an elephant joining together is against nature.

Do you know what the Bible says about people who turn away from the way God made them?[1]

> For although they knew God, they did not honor him as God or give thanks to him, but they became futile in their thinking, and their foolish hearts were darkened. Claiming to be wise, they became fools. (Romans 1:21–22)

1. See Romans 1:18–27.

The Bible says that they know who God is and what is right, but they don't respect God or thank Him. They don't worship Him as the God who made all things and who knows what is best for everything He has made. They don't thank Him for being good and wise and for making them the way He made them.

Instead, their thinking is mixed up, and their hearts are sinful. They want to follow their own way. They think their ideas are better than God's perfect design. But this is very foolish, sinful, and sad.[2] Only the God who made us knows what is best for us. His design for men and women is perfect. Who is smarter than

2. "Like many sins, homosexuality does not have to be learned. The child who never witnesses a temper tantrum can be proficient at throwing them; it is an instinctive ability of the human heart. Homosexuality is natural in the same way that anger or selfishness is natural. They are embedded in our fallen humanness. Indeed, homosexuality is 'natural,' but only in the sense that it is an expression of the sinful nature" (Ed Welch, *Blame It on the Brain* [Phillipsburg, NJ: P&R Publishing, 1998], 160–61).

God? Anyone who thinks he knows better than God does is very, very foolish and will only bring sadness into his life.

God made boys to be boys and girls to be girls. Boys are special, and girls are special too. It is not better to be a boy than a girl, or better to be a girl than a boy. Both are good. If you are a boy, God made you to be a boy, and that is very good. If you are a girl, God made you to be a girl, and that is very good too.

Some people think that you can decide whether you want to be a boy or a girl. Why is this foolish? God made you what you are even before you were born, and that is what is perfect for you. Trying to change what God made you is "claiming to be wise" but "becom[ing a] fool."

If you are a boy, you should honor or respect God as the all-wise Creator and say, "Thank You, God, for making me a boy. That is good, and You are good and wise." What do you think you should say and believe if God made you a girl?

When a boy wants to be a girl, he is fighting against God's good design for him. He is not "honor[ing] God or giv[ing] thanks to him." It is as foolish as a mouse saying, "I want to be a lion" and acting like a lion. Instead, a mouse should thank God that he is a mouse and should show the world that being a mouse is a good thing. A mouse shows the goodness of God when he squeezes into tiny spaces and runs fast. A lion shows the goodness of God when he roars and shakes his mane.

God does not make any mistakes. If you are a boy, God did a good thing. If you are a girl, God did a good thing. You can honor and thank Him by showing everyone how beautiful God's design is in making both boys and girls.

There are many people who do not believe that God's design is good. We need to pray for them and show them the beauty of God's good design for men and women. We need to show them the joy in being what God has made us—either a boy or a girl. How can you do that?

For you formed my inward parts;
    you knitted me together in my mother's womb.

I praise you, for I am fearfully and wonderfully made.
Wonderful are your works;

    my soul knows it very well. (Psalm 139:13–14)

LEARNING TO TRUST GOD

✢ Read Psalm 139:13–14 again. What do these verses tell you about the way you were made? What can you thank God for?

✢ Read Psalm 119:9–10. Verse 9 tells us how to please God and live rightly. How do we do this? What does "guarding it according to your word" mean? How can you seek God with your whole heart? The second part of verse 10 is a prayer. Pray this prayer each day this week.

✢ *Activity:* With your family, list ten good things about being a boy and ten good things about being a girl. Fathers, do an activity with your son that affirms his manhood; mothers, do an activity with your daughter that affirms her womanhood. Thank God for His good design in your life.[3]

3. Book recommendation: Joseph Nicolosi and Linda Ames Nicolosi, *A Parent's Guide to Preventing Homosexuality* (Downers Grove, IL: InterVarsity, 2002).

Recovering God's Good Design

Have you ever seen a baby try to eat by himself? What happens? Usually he makes a mess! He drops food on the floor and puts his hands in the bowl, and he often smears food all over the high chair tray and his face and hair. What a mess!

Can a baby clean up this mess by himself? No, he is not able. He needs the help of someone more skilled than he is.

We are in the same situation as the baby. We have made a mess of what God wants us to be as men and women. We have so distorted—twisted and mixed up—God's design for men and women that we can't fix it. What we need is the help of someone else—someone who understands our sinful hearts and can heal them.

That someone is Jesus. Only Jesus can forgive us. Only Jesus can change our hearts and heal our wrong ideas, attitudes, habits, and desires. We cannot do it on our own. We must trust Jesus fully. Do you know what it means to "trust"?

When a person jumps from a plane, he must trust his parachute to save him from crashing to the ground. In what ways must he trust his parachute?

He has to trust that the chute will open when he pulls the cord. He must trust that the parachute is in good condition and not full of holes. He has to trust that it is big and strong enough to hold his weight.

How does he show that he trusts his parachute? He jumps out of the plane.

This is what it means to trust Jesus. We must truly believe that He is the Savior who has paid for our sins and can change our hearts. We must know that His ways are right, and show that we believe this by obeying Him. By trusting and obeying what God says about manhood and womanhood, we will begin to become the men and women who God wants us to be.

Though you are a boy or a girl now, you will grow up and become a man or a woman. To become the man or woman God wants you to be, you must trust

Jesus and follow God's instructions about manhood and womanhood. You have to know and follow what God says about being a man or a woman with the help of Jesus.

What does it mean to be a man?[1] To be the man God wants you to be, you must have the heart and responsibility to kindly lead, provide for, and protect others, especially those in your family. To lead, a man must be a good example, jump in and do what must be done, and encourage others to do what is good

1. "At the heart of mature masculinity is a sense of benevolent responsibility to lead, provide for and protect" (John Piper and Wayne Grudem, *Recovering Biblical Manhood and Womanhood: A Response to Evangelical Feminism* [Wheaton: Crossway, 1991]. See Piper's full definition on page 36).

and right. God made men to provide for their families. A man must work hard to earn money to take care of his family. He must understand when his family members are sad and must help them to grow to love God more. When there is something dangerous or harmful, he must protect others and keep them safe. What are some ways that your dad does these things?

Not only must a man lead, provide for, and protect, but he must do it with kindness. So he listens to the ideas of others. Even when he must speak firmly, a godly man does it with kindness. He joyfully works for his family. He does not complain about his responsibilities, but gladly serves God and his family.

Does this sound like a hard job? It is. This is why a man must depend on Jesus and ask Him for strength. He must be strong to do what is right, be brave when things are hard, and be faithful to read the Bible and become wise. So if you want to grow to be a godly man, you must

Be watchful, stand firm in the faith, act like men, be strong. (1 Corinthians 16:13)

This means that you don't blame others when you are wrong, whine about doing your chores, or grumble about doing your homework. You don't hurt your sisters, but protect them and comfort them when they are sad. You trust Jesus to help you do the right thing and to encourage others to do what is right.

Some of you are girls and need to know what it means to be a true woman.[2] God made you to be content to support, accept, and encourage strength and leadership in a man. This means that a woman happily helps another to grow in leadership and strength. She understands that leaders are to be respected and that it is good to have leadership and to follow those in charge. She is happy to help and serve God and others.

If you want to grow to be a godly woman, Peter gives you some very good advice in the Bible.

2. "At the heart of mature femininity is a freeing disposition to affirm, receive and nurture strength and leadership" (ibid. See Piper's full definition on the same page).

Do not let your adorning be external—the braiding of hair and the putting on of gold jewelry, or the clothing you wear—but let your adorning be the hidden person of the heart with the imperishable beauty of a gentle and quiet spirit, which in God's sight is very precious. (1 Peter 3:3–4)

A girl who trusts Jesus is more concerned about having a beautiful heart than about looking beautiful on the outside. She wants to please God and help others.

Do you want to be a godly man or woman? Now is the time to trust Jesus and to start growing into the person He wants you to be.

LEARNING TO TRUST GOD

✛ Read 1 Peter 3:3–4 again. Explain what godly womanhood looks like in the life of a girl who is learning to follow God's good design.

✛ What kinds of strengths should a boy grow in now in order to become a godly man?

✛ *Activity:* Boys—talk with your dad about how you can start to practice leading, providing, and protecting your family. Take a practical step toward biblical manhood this week. Girls—talk with your mom about how you can start to practice supporting, encouraging, and helping. Take a practical step toward biblical womanhood this week.

Paul, an Example of Manhood

What would you do if you wanted to be a good pitcher? You would probably practice a lot. But there is something else you could do. Do you know what it is?

You would probably ask someone who is a good pitcher for some tips on how to pitch well. But the best way for a good pitcher to help you with your pitching is to show you how to pitch. When you watch what he does—how he moves his arm, holds the ball, and steps forward—you understand better how to pitch. You have a model, or example, to follow.

In the same way, if someone wants to know what being a godly man looks like, it is helpful to have an example to study and follow.

God has provided us with many examples of godly men in the Bible. For example, David was a "man after [God's] own heart" (1 Samuel 13:14) and he was also a great soldier, poet, and musician. Nehemiah was a great leader of others and a great builder! Joseph was a wise manager, and Daniel was a great advisor. These men of the Bible are all different and all did different work, yet they were all pleasing to God because they honored the Lord by loving Him and obeying His commands. Do you know some godly men?

The apostle Paul was another example of godly manhood. Paul was a brave and courageous missionary who spent his life leading, protecting, and providing for the needs of Christians in churches spread out across the known world. Even though Paul wasn't married, he followed God's design of male headship in his work as an apostle.

As an apostle, Paul took responsibility for protecting the church from false teachers—men who wanted to teach wrong things about God. He wrote many careful but bold letters to uncover the lies and tricks of those pretending to teach the truth. He traveled many miles on foot and by boat to teach in many churches.

He did this to encourage the Christians in these churches and to help them to grow strong in their faith.

Instead of getting paid for his work, Paul made and sold tents to take care of himself. But he also cared about the needs of others. He worked hard to encourage the churches to take care of the poor and those with other needs.

Paul did many good things to faithfully do the work that God had given him to do. But life wasn't easy for Paul. He had much suffering. Others didn't like what Paul did and made things harder for him. In a letter to the church at Corinth, Paul told about some of the hard things he had suffered.

Five times I received at the hands of the Jews the forty lashes less one. Three times I was beaten with rods. Once I was stoned. Three times I was shipwrecked; a night and a day I was adrift at sea; on frequent journeys, in danger from rivers, danger from robbers, danger from my own people,

danger from Gentiles, danger in the city, danger in the wilderness, danger at sea, danger from false brothers; in toil and hardship, through many a sleepless night, in hunger and thirst, often without food, in cold and exposure. And, apart from other things, there is the daily pressure on me of my anxiety for all the churches. (2 Corinthians 11:24–28)

Even though others tried to stop Paul, he worked tirelessly, faithfully, and courageously in obedience to Jesus. He did not get scared and run away like a coward. What was the secret of Paul's courage? His secret was trusting in Jesus and in His promises. He knew that Jesus promised to reward his work and bring him safely to heaven, no matter what difficulties he faced on earth.

Paul was not afraid to die. He trusted in Jesus, and he knew that when his work was done he would be with Jesus in heaven forever. He wrote this to the church in Corinth:

So we are always of good courage. We know that while we are at home in the body we are away from the Lord, for we walk by faith, not by sight. Yes, we are of good courage, and we would rather be away from the body and at home with the Lord. So whether we are at home or away, we make it our aim to please him. For we must all appear before the judgment seat of Christ, so that each one may receive what is due for what he has done in the body, whether good or evil. (2 Corinthians 5:6–10)

How did Paul keep doing the work that God gave him to do? Paul learned to have self-discipline so that he would not be lazy and unwilling to work. This is what Paul wrote about self-control:

Every athlete exercises self-control in all things. They do it to receive a perishable wreath, but we an imperishable. So I do not run aimlessly;

I do not box as one beating the air. But I discipline my body and keep it under control, lest after preaching to others I myself should be disqualified. (1 Corinthians 9:25–27)

Paul worked hard to develop self-control over his body so that he could work hard and be faithful to Christ until the end.

In all these things, the apostle Paul was a great example to all men. He himself encouraged others in the churches to follow his example and the example of others who lived like him.

Brothers, join in imitating me, and keep your eyes on those who walk according to the example you have in us. (Philippians 3:17)

Live like Paul, and you will know what it means to live as a godly man!

LEARNING TO TRUST GOD

✦ Read Hebrews 13:7. What kind of heroes, examples, and role models should we have? Why is it important to be careful in choosing those who we want to imitate?

✦ Are you careful about whom you spend time with? Do you spend time with those who are good examples or bad examples?

✦ *Activity:* As a family, read about other missionary heroes, such as David Brainerd, John Paton, Henry Martyn, William Carey, Adoniram Judson, and Jim Elliot. Discuss how they are great examples for us.

Jesus, the Perfect Example of Manhood

Do you know how great artists of the past like Michelangelo learned to make great paintings and sculptures? They learned to be good artists by copying the masters who had gone before them. Copying a master is an important way of learning.

In the same way, if a boy wants to learn how to be a man, he should learn to copy Jesus, the master of all things. Jesus is the perfect example of what it means to be a man. Jesus was much more than a man. He was the Son of God, but He was also fully a man. Both boys and girls should try to become more like Jesus, but boys have a special example to follow in Jesus for learning God's design for men.

Nobody knows what Jesus really looked like because there were no cameras when He lived, and no one drew or painted a picture of Him. Sometimes Jesus is painted in pictures in a girlish way, with long hair and soft looks. But the only way to understand what Jesus is truly like is to read the Bible, where the writers who knew Jesus recorded His words and actions.

In the Bible we see that Jesus was tough when He needed to be, as well as tender. He was called both "the lion of Judah" and also "the Lamb of God." He was also both a lion and a lamb in how He acted toward others—tough as well as tender, strong as well as gentle, bold as well as kind. He was perfect in every way and is the perfect example of manhood.

Do you remember when Jesus drove the money-changers out of the temple? This passage in the Bible records just how tough Jesus could be:

In the temple he found those who were selling oxen and sheep and pigeons, and the money-changers sitting there. And making a whip of cords, he drove them all out of the temple, with the sheep and oxen. And he poured out the coins of the money-changers and overturned their tables. And he told those who sold the pigeons, "Take these things away; do not make my Father's house a house of trade." His disciples remembered that it was written, "Zeal for your house will consume me." (John 2:14–17)

Jesus was tough on those who were dishonoring God, because Jesus loved His Father and wanted others to honor Him. Jesus was also tough when He talked to the Pharisees about their sin. He boldly told them that they were misleading the people. He was strong, He was forceful, and He said what needed to be said when He talked with them. Jesus was no wimp, that's for sure!

Even though Jesus was tough and strong, He was also kind and tender. As a man, He welcomed little children into His arms and blessed them. He cried with those who were weeping at the grave of Lazarus, and He treated the weak and those who were hurting with great kindness and compassion.[1] He always treated women with kindness and respect. In all these ways, Jesus has given us an example of kindness, gentleness, and tenderness.

1. See Mark 10:16; John 11:35; Matthew 9:36.

Jesus is also an example for men in faithfully doing the work that God gave Him. God gave Jesus a special job—to be the Savior. Jesus was determined to do the job that God gave Him, even though it was very hard. Adam had failed to do the work that God gave him, but Jesus was faithful to obey His Father. Jesus said, "My food is to do the will of him who sent me and to accomplish his work" (John 4:34). Doing what God sent Him to do was even more important to Jesus than eating. Do you think this way? This is a good example to us.

Jesus' work was something that only the Son of God could do—to obey His Father perfectly. God asked Him to give His life to save His people from their sin. In submitting to God's will and saving His people, Jesus became the greatest protector and provider of all.

Do you know what it cost Jesus to love His people by dying for them? Jesus suffered great pain on the cross. But He also suffered the greatest pain of having His Father turn away from Him. Jesus did all this to serve the people of God and to take care of their greatest need—the need for salvation. Even though Jesus is the King over all and had the power and authority to order others to serve Him, He came to serve them instead. Jesus was not like us. His words teach us how to follow Him.

You know that the rulers of the Gentiles lord it over them, and their great ones exercise authority over them. It shall not be so among you. But whoever would be great among you must be your servant, and whoever would be first among you must be your slave, even as the Son of Man came not to be served but to serve, and to give his life as a ransom for many. (Matthew 20:25–28)

What kind of leader was Jesus? Instead of ordering others to serve Him, Jesus became a servant-leader. He did not use His authority to serve Himself. Jesus is the perfect example for men to copy. Even though men are given a special role of headship and authority, they are to use it like Jesus did to serve others.

If I then, your Lord and Teacher, have washed your feet, you also ought to wash one another's feet. For I have given you an example, that you also should do just as I have done to you. Truly, truly, I say to you, a servant is not greater than his master, nor is a messenger greater than the one who sent him. If you know these things, blessed are you if you do them. (John 13:14–17)

LEARNING TO TRUST GOD

✛ Read Hebrews 12:1–2. What does it mean to be "looking to Jesus"? How can we keep our hearts and minds fixed on Jesus throughout the day?

✛ When does a man need to be tough? When does a man need to be tender? In what other ways does Jesus demonstrate the godly toughness and tenderness that all men should imitate?

✛ *Activity:* Pray that God would give the men in your life (your father, your brothers, yourself) the strength to be both tough and tender when needed, and the wisdom to know when to be which. With your dad, do something tough (participate in a prolife march, write a letter encouraging your leaders to do the right thing, take a stand on an important issue, etc.) or do something tender (visit someone in the hospital, help someone in need, etc.).

Wrong Thinking about Manhood

Wouldn't it be sad if a dog was confused about being a dog? Imagine a dog that did not know whether it should bark or meow or climb a tree. Imagine how sad it would be if it didn't know how to run, jump, and play as it was designed to do.

God wants to make sure that we are not confused about how men should live and act. In the Bible, the apostle Paul makes it very clear how godly men should behave.

> Older men are to be sober-minded, dignified, self-controlled, sound in faith, in love, and in steadfastness. . . . Likewise, urge the younger men to be self-controlled. Show yourself in all respects to be a model of good works, and in your teaching show integrity, dignity, and sound speech that cannot be condemned, so that an opponent may be put to shame, having nothing evil to say about us. (Titus 2:2, 6–8)

This is how men are to act—with self-control, faith, love, and sound speech. They are to be "a model of good works"—worth admiring and respecting in all things. Being a godly man is mostly about having godly character and submitting to God in all His ways.

There are other forms of "manliness" that may appear to be how a man should act. But, in the end, they really aren't true manliness.

Have you ever heard of fool's gold? Fool's gold looks like gold. It is yellow, sparkling, and shiny. It looks like the real thing, but it isn't. It is the mineral pyrite—"fake gold." Many people have mistaken fool's good for real gold and have been very disappointed. There is a true saying that "All that glitters is not gold." In the same way, there are many ideas about what a man should be that may seem right but are not. They are only fakes and not the real thing.

Some people think that, to be manly, one has to be a tough show-off who relies on himself, laughs at others, and rebelliously does whatever he pleases. Some think that true manhood involves things like driving a sports car, acting wild, or wearing a certain type of clothing, but this is not true manliness. It is as fake as fool's gold. This wrong idea of manhood is really a form of rebelliousness and pride, not true manliness. The Bible warns that "everyone who is arrogant in heart . . . will not go unpunished" and that "pride goes before destruction" (Proverbs 16:5, 18).

Others think that, to be manly, a man has to boss people around, bully others, and force others to do whatever he wants them to do. Is manliness being loud, rude, and quick-tempered? These things may all seem like true manliness, but they are only fake imitations. True manliness is self-controlled, patient, gentle, and slow to anger, as it says in Proverbs 16:32: "Whoever is slow to anger is better than the mighty, and he who rules his spirit than he who takes a city."

So does real manliness, being a truly godly man, mean that a man should always be nice, always agree with what others say, never upset anyone, and never

take a stand or make a decision that others don't agree with? No, this is being cowardly and a wimp. It is being a people-pleaser.

Do you know what it means to be a people-pleaser? A people-pleaser is someone who is more concerned about pleasing others than about pleasing God. A people-pleaser doesn't make his decisions based on what God wants him to do, but on what makes other people like him.

The Bible warns us about being a people-pleaser and tells us that we have to choose between serving God and serving another master.[1] If a person is living only to please others, he is not living to please God. Paul understood this when he wrote, "For am I now seeking the approval of man, or of God? Or am I trying to please man? If I were still trying to please man, I would not be a servant of Christ" (Galatians 1:10).

Being a people-pleasing "Mr. Nice Guy" is not what it means to be a truly godly man either. Becoming a godly man takes courage to do what is right even when others do not agree with you. It takes work, strength, courage, and self-discipline to grow into the kind of man who pleases God. This is what Paul wanted for Timothy when he said,

Train yourself for godliness; for while bodily training is of some value, godliness is of value in every way, as it holds promise for the present life and also for the life to come. The saying is trustworthy and deserving of full acceptance. For to this end we toil and strive, because we have our hope set on the living God. (1 Timothy 4:7–10)

1. See Matthew 6:24.

LEARNING TO TRUST GOD

✢ Read Titus 2:6–8 again. Why is self-control so important for young men? Without self-control, what will young men naturally do? How do you develop self-control?

✢ What is the difference between pleasing people and being a "people-pleaser"? In what ways are you tempted to be a people-pleaser? What fears are often behind the desire to be a people-pleaser?

✢ *Activity:* Memorize Titus 2:6–8. (Girls can memorize this verse too, because it is also important for girls to know what godly manhood looks like.) How can you be a model of good works? What is a "good work" that you and your family can do this week?

Ruth, an Example of Womanhood

Suppose you had to draw a picture of a horse. What would make it easier to draw? If you had an example or model to show you what a horse looks like, you could copy it.

God has given us many examples in the Bible of womanhood to copy. One of those models is Ruth. Ruth was from the land of Moab. The Moabites didn't love God, but God had sent a Jewish woman named Naomi and her husband and two sons from Israel to Moab. One of her sons married Ruth. Later, he and his father and brother all died. So Naomi decided to go back to Israel.

But Ruth would not let Naomi go back alone.

Do not urge me to leave you or to return from following you. For where you go I will go, and where you lodge I will lodge. Your people shall be my people, and your God my God. (Ruth 1:16)

What does this tell you about Ruth? She was loyal and kind. Ruth did not want Naomi, who was old, to be alone. Ruth wanted to stay with her and help her. She was a companion, or friend and helper to Naomi just as God had created women to be. But more importantly, Ruth loved Naomi's God. So she left her people to be with the people of God.

Ruth worked hard in Israel to provide for Naomi and herself. She gathered the grain that was left for poor people in the fields. She worked continually, stopping only for a short rest. A man named Boaz owned one of the fields where Ruth gathered grain, and he noticed Ruth. His workers told him who Ruth was and how hard she worked. Boaz was a relative of Naomi and knew that Ruth was faithfully caring for Naomi.

Then Boaz said to Ruth, "Now, listen, my daughter, do not go to glean in another field or leave this one, but keep close to my young women." (Ruth 2:8)

How was Boaz an example of biblical manhood? He was a leader who took responsibility for Ruth. He saw Ruth's problem and worked to solve it for her. He protected her by inviting her to stay in his field with his workers. He also provided for her by giving her the leftover grain. Boaz saw that Ruth was a godly woman who was faithful to help Naomi and work hard. He knew she had given up much so that she could take care of Naomi.

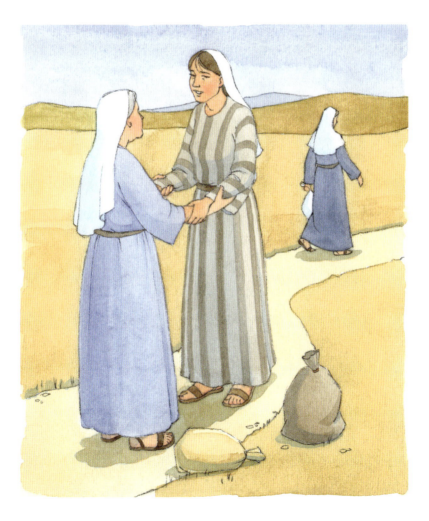

Boaz treated Ruth with kindness. He gave her bread and corn to eat for lunch. He also told his workers to help Ruth by pulling some grain from the bundles to leave for her and instructed them not to bother her. He knew that Ruth would be safe in his fields.

Ruth told Naomi about Boaz's kindness to her. Naomi knew that Boaz was a godly man and would be a good leader, provider, and protector for Ruth. Naomi decided that Boaz would be a good husband for Ruth, so she told Ruth how to let Boaz know that she wanted him to marry her.

What do you think Ruth thought about Naomi's plan? What do you think she said to Naomi? She didn't say, "How dare you pick a husband for me. I don't have to listen to you! You can't run my life." Ruth was a godly woman who gladly submitted to Naomi. She trusted Naomi and listened to her advice.

And she replied, "All that you say I will do." (Ruth 3:5)

Ruth trusted God and followed His ways. She also trusted Boaz to care for her.

I am Ruth, your servant. Spread your wings over your servant, for you are a redeemer. (Ruth 3:9)

A redeemer was a close relative who could rescue a woman whose husband had died, by marrying her to keep her from being poor and alone. Boaz did this for Ruth because he saw that she was a "worthy woman"—a godly woman who loved God and would be a helper and companion.

So Boaz married Ruth and, in time, they had a son. His name was Obed, and there was great rejoicing when he was born. Naomi now had a grandson! She was not alone, but had a family again. Ruth was a wife and a mother.

But something even greater was happening. God was blessing Ruth, a Moabite who loved God, with being part of His great plan to send a Savior. Obed was the father of Jesse, who was the father of King David. And from King David and his son and that son's son . . . and the son that came after that, and the following sons . . . came Jesus, the Savior of the world, who rescued His people from sin and separation from God.

Would you like to be a woman like Ruth, or be like Boaz and marry a woman like Ruth? Love God, trust Jesus, and follow God's ways. There is great joy when we obey God and love His design!

LEARNING TO TRUST GOD

✚ Read Ruth 2. In what ways did Ruth follow God? How did God bless her? What did Boaz appreciate about Ruth?

✚ Ask your dad what qualities he appreciates about your mother. Girls: How can you be a young woman like this? Boys: What are some good qualities a boy should encourage in girls he knows?

✚ *Activity:* As a family, talk about how the story of Ruth and Boaz is like Jesus and His people. What has Jesus done for Christians? How can we respond to Jesus like Ruth responded to Naomi and Boaz? Make a booklet explaining the gospel, and share it with someone.

Mary and Sarah, Examples of Womanhood

What do you do when your plans don't work out? Do you whine, grumble, or complain? Do you get mad? We would all like to say that we have a good attitude because we trust God to know what is best. But sadly, that isn't always the way it is. If you plan to go bike riding but it rains, what might you say or do? If you want to play a computer game but your mother tells you to do your homework, what is your attitude?

We all have disappointments, and what we do about them shows what is in our hearts. Mary had a disappointment too—a very big disappointment. Mary was not married, but Joseph had asked her to be his wife. Mary was probably happy to think of marrying Joseph and spending her life with him. But then something happened that was not part of Mary's plan.

God sent an angel to Mary. This was certainly very unusual! But even more unusual was the message that the angel gave to Mary.

And the angel said to her, "Do not be afraid, Mary, for you have found favor with God. And behold, you will conceive in your womb and bear a son, and you shall call his name Jesus. He will be great and will be called the Son of the Most High." (Luke 1:30–32)

Mary was going to have a baby? How could this be? Mary knew that God's Word says only married people should have babies. It would not be right for her and Joseph to have a child before they were married. And how could Joseph's son be called the Son of the Most High? That couldn't be.

Then the angel told her that Joseph would not be the father. God Himself would be the father. Mary would give birth to the Son of God! That is very good news for the world and for people like you and me. But what about Mary? Was it good news for her?

Surely she needed a Savior too, but what would people think of her? People would not believe that her baby was the Son of God. They would think she had sinned with some man and had his baby. They would be mean to her, and she would have no one to provide for her. She would be poor, and it would be hard to care for her baby alone. Could she even be a good mother to the Son of God? What would Joseph think? He would think she had been unfaithful and would not marry her. What about all her dreams and plans?

But even though all those problems were real, there was something more important to Mary.

And Mary said, "Behold, I am the servant of the Lord; let it be to me according to your word." And the angel departed from her. (Luke 1:38)

Mary knew who she was. She was God's servant. His plans were more important than hers. She trusted God and submitted to His plans for her. The suffering that would come to her was less important than following God.

Mary is an example of a true woman who trusts God. She trusted God by accepting His plans for her life without complaining. She truly believed that God is wise and good and that His plans are always right.

Sarah was another woman who trusted God. She was married to Abraham. When God called Abraham to leave his home and go to a strange land, Sarah submitted to Abraham and went with him. She trusted God, who had given her Abraham as her husband and leader. She did not insist on her way and was not afraid to trust God's plan. This is why the Bible tells us to be like Sarah.

But let your adorning be the hidden person of the heart with the imperishable beauty of a gentle and quiet spirit, which in God's sight is very precious. For this is how the holy women who hoped in God used to adorn themselves, by submitting to their own husbands, as Sarah obeyed Abraham, calling him lord. And you are her children, if you do good and do not fear anything that is frightening. (1 Peter 3:4–6)

Sarah had a "gentle and quiet spirit." Her heart was peaceful as she trusted God. Instead of getting upset and trying to be in charge, or arguing, she had a beautiful trust in God—a trust that God said is very precious. A woman with a "gentle and quiet spirit" does not insist on her own way and is not pushy and demanding. Instead, she depends on God for all she needs.

Because Sarah trusted God, she knew that His ways are good and right. She knew it was right to respect and trust her husband too. The Bible says that she obeyed Abraham and called him "lord."

Does your mother call your father "lord"? Women don't call their husbands "lord" anymore, but they can show the same kind of respect to their husbands that Sarah showed to Abraham. They can speak with respect, honor his decisions, want to please their husbands, and teach their children to respect their father.

Today, you and all girls can be like Sarah and can "do good and do not fear" because your trust is in God. Like Mary, you can be God's servant and submit to His plans. You can rejoice in God's good design for women.

LEARNING TO TRUST GOD

✛ Read Luke 1:46–55. How can you tell from Mary's words that she trusted God and that God's plan was more important to her than her plan?

✛ Read Genesis 12:10–20. How did Sarai (Sarah) honor Abram (Abraham)? How was God faithful to Abram and Sarai? What does this tell you about who God is?

✛ *Activity:* Gladys Aylward lived in London in the early 1900s. She had two great sorrows as a young girl—that she had black hair and that she was short. With your family, look up the plan that God had for Gladys's life. Why did God make her short and give her black hair? When Gladys Aylward arrived in China, she looked around at the people. "'Every single one of them,' she said, 'had black hair. And every single one of them had stopped growing when I did. And I said, "Lord God, You know what you're doing!"'"[1] Can God be trusted with your life, dreams, and plans? Does He really know what is best? Does it really pay to walk in His ways? What is something that you need to trust God with? Can you give that problem to God? Pray with your family for a trusting heart like Mary and Sarah had.

1. Elisabeth Elliot, *Let Me Be a Woman* (Carol Stream, IL: Tyndale House, 1976), 23.

Wrong Thinking about Womanhood

If you were eating a bowl of soup, would you use a fork? Why not? To use a fork to eat soup would go against the design of the fork. A fork wasn't made for scooping soup. But a spoon was made for scooping and works well for eating soup.

Just as it is foolish to go against the design of spoons and forks, it is foolish to go against God's design for men and women. It doesn't work, and it brings much unhappiness. A baby might try to use a fork to eat soup because a baby doesn't understand about forks and spoons. And sometimes people don't follow God's design because they don't really understand God's design. Some people think God's idea of womanhood means that women are always bossed around, that they can't have any ideas or responsibilities of their own, and that they are weak and afraid. But this isn't what the Bible says about womanhood.

The book of Proverbs helps us to understand God's idea of womanhood.

An excellent wife who can find?
    She is far more precious than jewels.
The heart of her husband trusts in her,

. . . .

She does him good, and not harm,
    all the days of her life. (Proverbs 31:10–12)

The Bible says that a godly wife is precious—even more precious than diamonds. Her husband trusts her. He knows that she has many abilities, and he appreciates who she is and what she does.

She seeks wool and flax,
    and works with willing hands.

. . . .

She considers a field and buys it;
    with the fruit of her hands she plants a vineyard.

. . . .

She makes linen garments and sells them;

. . . .

She looks well to the ways of her household
    and does not eat the bread of idleness. (Proverbs 31:13, 16, 24, 27)

What can you tell about this woman from these verses? She is a hard and cheerful worker; she isn't lazy and doesn't try to get out of work. Instead of wasting her time on silly things, she is helpful. She makes good decisions. She can be trusted to buy a field and plan out a vineyard where grapes are grown. This is a woman with good ideas, and she doesn't just think about them—she does them!

A gorilla is strong. Lions are strong. Many men are strong. Are true women strong? Yes, but they are strong in a different way.

She dresses herself with strength
    and makes her arms strong.

. . . .

She is not afraid of snow for her household,
    for all her household are clothed in scarlet.

. . . .

Strength and dignity are her clothing,
    and she laughs at the time to come. (Proverbs 31:17, 21, 25)

What kind of strength does a godly woman have? Not a gorilla kind of strength, but a different kind of strength. She has the strength to do what is right, the strength to trust God to care for her, and the strength not to fear what might happen. She doesn't think about the days to come and say, "Oh no; what if something bad happens? I am so afraid." She knows that God will help her with whatever happens.

She opens her hand to the poor
    and reaches out her hands to the needy.

. . . .

She opens her mouth with wisdom,
    and the teaching of kindness is on her tongue. (Proverbs 31:20, 26)

Not only does a godly woman take care of her own family, but she is also kind to others. When she sees pain and suffering, her heart is compassionate and she wants to help. She is not selfish but is generous and ready to share with others. She has money and things to share because she is a good helper and a wise woman.

Do you think it would be easy to love a woman like this? How do you think her children and husband feel about her?

Her children rise up and call her blessed;
  her husband also, and he praises her:
"Many women have done excellently,
  but you surpass them all." (Proverbs 31:28–29)

"Surpass" means to be better than the rest—to be the best. Her family loves her and knows she is a great treasure—"far more precious than jewels."

Do you know what is the most famous diamond in the world? It is the Hope Diamond. It is a large, bluish-colored diamond stored in a museum in Washington, D.C. What do you think this famous diamond is worth? It is worth more than 250 million dollars! That is lots and lots of money! But a godly woman, a true woman, is worth much more than even the Hope Diamond!

Don't you wish that every woman loved God's good design for women? They would be like beautiful diamonds.

Charm is deceitful, and beauty is vain,
but a woman who fears the LORD is to be praised. (Proverbs 31:30)

LEARNING TO TRUST GOD

✤ Read Proverbs 31:30 again. What do the words "charm" and "vain" mean? Is it wrong to try to look nice? What is this verse saying about true beauty?

✤ Read Proverbs 31:10–31. What makes this woman beautiful?

✤ *Activity:* As a family, think of a woman you know who is like the woman in Proverbs 31. Then do something to bless this woman. Pray for the girls and women who you know, and ask God to make them true Proverbs 31 women.

The Blessing of Purity

Have you ever seen an explosion caused by dynamite? Dynamite is so powerful that it can blast a hole in the side of a mountain or bring a whole building crashing to the ground. Dynamite is powerful and wonderfully strong for those who build roads and need to move heavy rocks out of the way. Although dynamite can be very useful, it is dangerous. It must be handled with great care and used only for good.

In the same way, the desires that men and women have to love and enjoy each other are powerful and good, and yet they can be harmful and destructive if they are not handled with care and used as God has designed them. Men and women were designed by God to love, enjoy, and be attracted to each other. This attraction can give them the desire to hug, kiss, look at, touch, and be close to each other. These desires can be a powerful force—like dynamite—especially as boys and girls grow into adults.

While these God-given desires are good, they are also dangerous and must be handled with great care! God has said that only a married man and woman—only a husband and a wife—should look at and touch each others' bodies in a close and personal way. Only within marriage can a man and a woman fully enjoy and be close to each other in a way that honors God and is not destructive.

Do you remember the story of Joseph and Potiphar's wife? Joseph was trusted to watch over Potiphar's house, but Potiphar's wife was attracted to Joseph. She wanted Joseph to treat her as only her husband should. Joseph refused. He said to her, "How [could] I do this great wickedness and sin against God?" (Genesis 39:9). One day when her husband was not around, Potiphar's wife grabbed Joseph by his cloak. Instead of staying with her and treating her like his wife, Joseph ran out of the house in order to escape the evil that she was tempting him to do.[1]

1. See Genesis 39:12.

Joseph did the right thing by *running away* from temptation and sin. Running away from temptation is something we all need to learn to do and something we can do only with the help and grace of God. Joseph knew that he could not stay in the house with Potiphar's wife and stay pure. He ran away to keep himself from the dirtiness and wrongness of sin and to keep himself pure.

Purity is more than just having pure or right actions. Purity is also having pure thoughts and desires. If a person has sinful thoughts and desires, he has sinned in his heart, even if he has not done sinful actions. This is what Jesus taught when He said,

> You have heard that it was said, "You shall not commit adultery." But I say to you that everyone who looks at a woman with lustful intent has already committed adultery with her in his heart. (Matthew 5:27–28)

Having impure or "lustful" looks, desires, or imaginations about someone else is a type of sin that often leads to further sin. Jesus warns that we must take these types of sins seriously. We must cut out anything from our lives that might lead us to sin in this way.

> If your right eye causes you to sin, tear it out and throw it away. For it is better that you lose one of your members than that your whole body be thrown

into hell. And if your right hand causes you to sin, cut it off and throw it away. For it is better that you lose one of your members than that your whole body go into hell. (Matthew 5:29–30)

If something is leading us into impurity, like wrong thoughts and feelings about a girl or a boy, it should be cut off. Even if it feels like a part of us, like an eye or a hand, it should be cut off to keep us from falling into sin. This means we should cut out of our lives whatever movies, TV programs, websites, books, and friendships are encouraging us to sin.

To help others fight sinful desires, both boys and girls need to be modest and not be a show-off or do things that draw attention to themselves or their bodies. This means not dressing or acting in a way that encourages sinful thoughts and desires in others.

Paul says that women "should adorn themselves in respectable apparel, with modesty and self-control" (1 Timothy 2:9). Being modest is mostly an attitude in the heart. It is part of having self-control. But it is also a matter of how girls behave around boys, how boys behave around girls, and even what clothing we wear.

The reason to be pure as boys and girls, or men and women, is so that we can glorify and enjoy more and more of God and His goodness to us. Just as a fence keeps a small child away from the danger of the street, God has put fences or boundaries around our desires. When we stay inside God's purity fence, we can have great joy. Jesus Himself gave us the promise that those who are pure in heart will find the blessing of God, when He said,

"Blessed are the pure in heart, for they shall see God." (Matthew 5:8)

LEARNING TO TRUST GOD

✦ Read Matthew 23:25–28. What sin is Jesus pointing out? How is this a warning for us?

✦ What tempts you to impurity and sin? Are there patterns of behavior (TV, Internet, magazines) that you need to flee from?

✦ *Activity:* Discuss with your parents how to appropriately dress and interact with members of the opposite gender. Sometime this week, go to a public place with your parents and notice the behavior between boys and girls. Talk about what is appropriate and what is not.

Honoring Each Other

There is a right and a wrong way to meet royalty. What do you think is the proper way to meet the Queen of England? Most of us don't know the correct manners to meet the queen. But some of those manners include standing when the queen enters the room, not speaking unless she speaks to you, and greeting her as "Your Majesty" or "Your Royal Highness." Oh, and if the queen puts out her hand, you should never kiss it or give her a firm handshake. You should only quickly touch her hand.

There are also some things you should never do—like chew gum, slap her on the back, put your arm around her, or give her a hug. She is royalty, not a pal.

Just as there is an appropriate way to treat a queen, there is a right way for girls and boys and men and women to treat each other. When we do things the right way, we are less likely to hurt each other.

Where can we find out about the right way to treat each other? In the Bible, the only trustworthy guide. The Bible tells us that Christians are to be like a family to each other.[1]

> Do not rebuke an older man but encourage him as you would a father, younger men as brothers, older women as mothers, younger women as sisters, in all purity. (1 Timothy 5:1–2)

How should Christian men and women and boys and girls treat each other? They should treat each other as brothers and sisters. You might sometimes fight with your brother or sister, but this is not what the Bible is talking about! Even if you sometimes fight, you have a deep concern for each other. You want what is best for each other and will always care for each other.

1. See 1 Timothy 3:15.

These verses also tell us to treat each other "in all purity." This means we have to be careful. We have to protect each other's thoughts, hearts, and bodies. We don't want to do anything that will hurt other people's faith or cause them to disobey God's commands.

The Bible also tells us about a way we are supposed to "outdo one another."

Love one another with brotherly affection. Outdo one another in showing honor. (Romans 12:10)

Do you know what it means to "outdo one another"? It means that we try to be the best. It is like the word *surpass*, which we learned earlier. Boys should respect who God made girls to be, and girls should respect who God made boys

to be. We are different, but both are good and deserve respect. If everyone tried to be the best at honoring and respecting each other and treating each other right, wouldn't that be great?

There are lots of ways we can treat each other that are dishonoring. Can you think of some? It is not honoring to make fun of each other or to call each other names. Treating someone unkindly or embarrassing someone is not honoring. Forcing someone to do something that he thinks is wrong is also dishonoring.

Some boys make fun of girls because they might cry more easily than boys do, or because girls talk and giggle a lot, but this is part of what girls are like. Girls may also make fun of boys. Boys like to wrestle and are usually louder than girls, but that isn't a reason for girls to think that they are better than boys. Boys are just being boys, like God made them to be.

Let's think about two kinds of boys. One boy greets a girl who he knows by slapping her on the back like he does to his buddies. When she cries out, he says, "Aw, don't be such a sissy." He then races to get the only seat left in the room. The second boy sees what happened and greets the girl. He gets up from his chair and asks if she would like to sit there. Which boy was respectful of the girl? The second boy treated her with special honor just because she is a girl. He did not embarrass or make fun of her. He treated her politely and protected her. Even though he wanted a chair, he knows that men are to make sacrifices for others. He did what was right.

Now let's talk about two kinds of girls. One girl sees a boy she knows jumping off the monkey bars. She yells, "Stop that! You are going to get hurt!" When he falls and scrapes his knee, she says, "I told you that would happen. Now go wash the blood off your knee. Then play on the swings with me." The second girl sees the same thing, and when the boy falls she offers him a tissue to wipe his knee. She says, "I am sorry you got hurt. But that was a good trick. You were brave to try it." Then she asks if he wants to play a game with her. When he pulls her out of the way of another jumping boy, she thanks him. Which girl treated the boy with honor?

The second girl honored the boy. She understood that he is different from her and that God made him to take risks and be strong and brave. She did not try to boss him around or control him. She politely asked if he wanted to do something. When he pulled her out of the way, she did not tell him that she could take care of herself. Instead, she was grateful for his protection and that he treated her special.

You may not see many girls and boys treating each other with honor. But you can be an example of following God's good design. With God's help you can "outdo" others in showing honor.

Love one another with brotherly affection. Outdo one another in showing honor. (Romans 12:10)

LEARNING TO TRUST GOD

✢ Read Ephesians 4:29. What does it say about how you can honor each other? With your mom or dad, think of a few examples of both the wrong and the right kinds of speech.

✢ What sins keep us from honoring one another? Why do you need God?

✢ *Activity:* With your family, talk about how you can honor each other. This week, practice showing honor to members of the opposite gender in your family, church, and school.

Marriage and Singleness

Can you name some wedding gifts? Someone might give a towel and washcloth. Another might give a frying pan. Is one gift better than the other? They are both good gifts. One isn't better than the other. They are just different from each other.

If you had to wash your face, you would be glad for a towel and washcloth. You can't dry your face with a pan! But you can't cook supper in a towel either! So both gifts are good.

Being married and being single (not married) are gifts too. Both are good gifts from God. One isn't better than the other. They are just different from each other.

We have already learned that God made marriage and said "it is not good that the man should be alone" (Genesis 2:18). The Bible also says,

> He who finds a wife finds a good thing
> and obtains favor from the LORD. (Proverbs 18:22)

So being married is a blessing—a good thing—from God. But in order for marriage to bring the greatest happiness, it must follow God's design. We already know that men and women (and boys and girls) are to honor one another. God also has some special instructions about marriage.

> Have you not read that he who created them from the beginning made them male and female, and said, "Therefore a man shall leave his father and his mother and hold fast to his wife, and the two shall become one flesh"? So they are no longer two but one flesh. What therefore God has joined together, let not man separate. (Matthew 19:4–6)

Can you see God's instructions in these verses? You may need to read them again. Here are some hints.

- Who created man and woman? [God] Since God created us, He knows the best design for us.
- What two people make a marriage? [a man and a woman] Marriage is not between a man and a man, or a woman and a woman. It is only between a man and a woman. Some people want to change marriage so that two men or two women can be married, but this is not God's design and it is wrong.
- Who joins a man and a woman in marriage? [God] God Himself makes them one—one pair, one family, one partnership.
- What should not be done to what God has joined together? [not be separated, split, or parted] God's design is for marriage to last until death. A marriage should not end until one person dies.

What shape works best for a wheel? A circle is the best design for a wheel because it rolls easily. A square or triangle with sharp corners would not work well at all!

It is the same with marriage. There is a best design. Marriage works best when God's design is used. God is wise and loving. He always gives instructions or commands for our good. He said that marriage is to last for a person's whole life. Sometimes people don't want to be husband and wife anymore so they decide to end their marriage. This is called divorce, and it is not God's design. God says that He "hates divorce." Why do you think God hates divorce? He hates it because He joined the man and woman together, and He knows that separating brings much sorrow and pain. Marriage is meant to be an example of God's faithfulness to His people. So divorce in marriage is not showing God's good example to others.

God has another command about marriage. Christians are only to marry Christians. A Christian must not marry someone who does not love and serve God. That is God's way. It is the best and happiest way. The Bible says,

Do not be unequally yoked together with unbelievers. For what partnership has righteousness with lawlessness? Or what fellowship has light with darkness? (2 Corinthians 6:14)

The Bible also talks about being single. This is what Paul said:

I wish that all were as I myself am. But each has his own gift from God, one of one kind and one of another. To the unmarried and the widows I say that it is good for them to remain single as I am. (1 Corinthians 7:7–8).

Paul is saying it is good to be single. But how can marriage and singleness both be good? They have different purposes—like towels and pans have different purposes. Just as there are good things about being married—like leadership, provision, protection, friendship, and helping—there are good things about being single.

Single people have more freedom. They don't have a husband or wife or children who depend on them. They can spend more time serving God and helping others. They depend on God more, rather than on another person, so they can have a closer relationship with God.

So which is better—being married or single? What is best is whatever God wants for you. He has a plan for you that is perfect. He has a plan for the world and He knows the best thing for you in His plan. He has a special purpose just for you.

But the most important thing of all is not whether you are married or single. The most important thing is if you are a child of God. This is best of all! God has a promise for all His children, both the married and the single.

> For your Maker is your husband, the LORD of hosts is his name; and the Holy One of Israel is your Redeemer, the God of the whole earth he is called. (Isaiah 54:5)

LEARNING TO TRUST GOD

✦ Read 1 Corinthians 7:32–34. What are married people concerned about? What does Paul say is good about being single?

✦ Read Isaiah 54:5 again. What does this verse call God? What do these names tell you about God? How is God like a husband to His people? Why is God the best husband?

✦ *Activity:* If we don't look at things the way God does, we might think it is better to be married than single. Sometimes people do not serve or honor single people. As a family, do something this week to bless a single person.

Husbands and Fathers

Do you know what gravity is? Gravity is a force God made that pulls things back to earth. When you throw a ball up, does it keep going up? What happens? It falls down because gravity pulls it down. Ripe apples fall down from a tree, not up, because of gravity.

Can you make the apple fall up instead of down? You might be able to throw it up, but then it will fall down. You cannot change God's law of gravity. It is unchangeable. God's laws are like this. Even if we don't like them, we can't change them.

Just as God's laws for gravity are unchangeable, so are God's laws about the best way that a family works. God's design for husbands and wives and families is perfect. He gave us instructions or commands that show us His design. We can disobey God's commands, but there are always consequences or problems when we do that.

God's design is very clear.

But I want you to understand that the head of every man is Christ, the head of a wife is her husband, and the head of Christ is God. (1 Corinthians 11:3)

This is easy to understand. God is in charge of all things including Christ (Jesus). Jesus is in charge or is the head of the husband. And the husband is the head or the leader of the wife. This doesn't mean that the husband is better than the wife. He just has a different role or job than she does.

God's command is clear, so we can't say that we don't understand God's ways. Disobedience usually comes from not *wanting* to follow God's law. It comes from a sinful heart.

Many times a husband has another important role—to be a father. A good father provides for, protects, and leads his children. His wife helps him with his job, but he has the main responsibility because his job is to be the head. And he must do this job in a special way.

> Fathers, do not provoke your children to anger, but bring them up in the discipline and instruction of the Lord. (Ephesians 6:4)

This does not mean that a father should never do anything that upsets his children or makes them angry. It means that he should not be sinful in the way he treats his children. He should not treat his children badly so that they get angry. He should not be mean, unfair, or overly controlling. He should not pick on them or break his promises. Fathers should admit their sin and ask for forgiveness. They should make good decisions and give good instructions. It would be sinful for a father to ignore his children, not provide for them, or fail to do his jobs at home.

Instead, fathers should bless or do good to their children. Most importantly, a father should "bring them up in the discipline and instruction of the Lord." Do you know what that means? It means that he should teach them about God and His ways. When children are sinful, fathers should correct them and teach them what is right. When they need to be punished, he should punish them kindly, for their good. Because you and all children were born with a sinful heart,[1] you need faithful parents to discipline your sinful heart and to tell you about Jesus, who forgives and changes sinful hearts.

Being a father is a big job! So it is important to pray for your father.[2] Pray that he will depend on God to help him to be a good father. Pray that he will faithfully teach and discipline you. Pray that he will lead his family in an *active, loving,* and *sacrificial* way. This is the way that God wants him to lead.

Let's see what the words *active, loving,* and *sacrificial* mean.

Active: The Bible does not say that husbands can choose or decide if they want to be the head of the home. It says they are the head of the home. They must jump in and do it. They have to be active or take action. They must fight laziness, fear, and selfishness. They must pay attention to their families and should not make excuses for failing to lead. Pray that your dad is active in taking leadership and fighting sin.

Loving: Husbands and fathers are to treat their families the same way that Jesus treats His people—lovingly or with kindness.[3] Jesus loved the church and died for His people. Being harsh and unloving is not like Jesus. Husbands and fathers must understand that women are different from men, and that children are not grown-ups and have much to learn. Pray that God would help your father to be loving and to lead his family with kindness, patience, and gentleness.

1. See Genesis 6:5; Psalm 51:5; Jeremiah 17:9.
2. If you are a single mother reading this with your child, it is suggested that you explain to your child that you must do the job of father and mother. So you are especially in need of your child's prayers.
3. See Ephesians 5:25–30; Colossians 3:18–19; 1 Peter 3:7.

Sacrificial: Jesus gave up so much for the church. He gave His life. God asks husbands and fathers to be unselfish. This means that they must make sacrifices and give up their own wants to care for their families.[4] A father might have to give up something that he likes to do, or spend money he does not want to spend. He might have to give up his plans, or sometimes even his life, for his family. Pray that your father will follow Jesus' example and be sacrificial and give up his desires joyfully.

Can you do this for your father? You can help him with his hard job by praying for him to be a leader, provider, and protector who is active, loving, and sacrificial. That's your job!

LEARNING TO TRUST GOD

✦ Read Ephesians 5:25. What is the model for the relationship between a husband and a wife? How does Jesus treat us?

✦ In what ways does your father sacrifice for your family? Have you thanked him for this? How can you show that you appreciate what he does for you?

✦ *Activity:* As a family, pray for your husband/father.[5] Then do something special for Dad this week. Optional: find out where the phrase "Women and children first" started. Hint: look up the HMS *Birkenhead* and Lieutenant-Colonel Seton.

---

4. See Ephesians 5:25.
5. You may want to pray Isaiah 40:10 for your father regularly.

Wives and Mothers

Have you ever seen a trapeze act?[1] The acrobats swing high above the ground. Sometimes a woman acrobat has to jump from her swing to be caught by a man acrobat. She has to trust him to catch her. If he misses, she will fall.

Do you think the man ever makes a mistake? Yes, he does. So why does she trust him? She trusts him because she knows that most of the time he doesn't make a mistake—and because she knows there is a net below that will catch her if he makes a mistake.

This is the same way for a wife. She submits to her husband and trusts that he will care for her and make good decisions. But sometimes husbands make mistakes. So how can a godly woman still lovingly submit to her husband?

She can follow her husband because she has a "safety net." God is her "safety net." He will always provide, protect, and lead her. He will always work for her good. She knows that God never makes mistakes, and He rules over all things. A godly woman trusts God, so she is able to trust the husband who God gave to her.[2]

A wife who trusts God and is respectful is a good example to a husband who may not be obeying God's Word.

Likewise, wives, be subject to your own husbands, so that even if some do not obey the word, they may be won without a word by the conduct of their wives, when they see your respectful and pure conduct. (1 Peter 3:1–2)

It is not easy for a woman to follow and respect a husband who is disobedient. She must depend on God. He will give her the grace and strength to do what is right.

1. If your child has not seen a trapeze act, you may want to view one on the Internet before reading the story. (Try doing an Internet search on "North Korean flying trapeze.")

2. Note: A wife is never to follow her husband into sin. Ultimately, her submission is first and foremost to Christ.

God has given women another important work. Do you know what that is? It is having children and caring for them.[3] God specially designed women to provide a safe place for babies to grow until they are born. But that is only part of the special job that God has given women.

Mothers and fathers both care for their children, but women have a special ability. They have a special way that men don't have of caring for children. How is the way that your mother cares for you different from the way that your father cares for you?

Both mothers and fathers help children to grow up in good ways. Dads often like to tumble and play with their children. Moms often like to ask questions and talk with their children. Mothers help their children to feel protected by cuddling them. Fathers help their children to try new things like climbing on the monkey bars and exploring new places.

Usually when children are little mothers spend more time with them than fathers do, who often have to go to work every day. So mothers have many chances to guide the way that their children think and behave and what kind of person they are becoming. This is a really important job. Even women who don't have children of their own can join in this special job that God has given women. They can care for the children of others, teach Sunday school, or work in the church nursery.

3. See 1 Timothy 2:15.

This is one of the most important jobs a woman can do. The kind of people we become will help make the world either better or worse. Ahaziah was a king of Judah. What kind of mother do you think he had?

Ahaziah was twenty-two years old when he began to reign, and he reigned one year in Jerusalem. His mother's name was Athaliah, the granddaughter of Omri. He also walked in the ways of the house of Ahab, for his mother was his counselor in doing wickedly. (2 Chronicles 22:2–3)

The Bible says that Ahaziah "did what was evil in the sight of the Lord" (2 Chronicles 22:4). He did evil things like the wicked King Ahab had done. What is one reason the Bible gives for why Ahaziah was so wicked? He listened to his mother, who gave him evil advice. His mother did not love God or teach her son to honor God. She did not lead him to do what is right. She was not faithful to do the important job that God had given her.

Timothy's mother, Lois, and his grandmother, Eunice, were not like Ahaziah's mother. They were godly women who faithfully taught Timothy about God. Timothy grew up to be a godly man and a great leader in the church. What job could be more important than helping children to grow up right?

Can you see that being a wife and a mother is a blessing God has given to women? They have great influence for either good or evil.[4] They may either be like Athaliah or like Lois. Women can make a happy home and can take care of the needs of their families, or they can make everyone unhappy as they grumble about the jobs they have to do at home. It is a great privilege for a woman to be a

4. Note the following inspirational section from a sermon by Edward T. Sullivan: "'The great events of this world,' says someone, 'are not battles and earthquakes and hurricanes. The great events of this world are babies. They are earthquakes and hurricanes.' . . . Oh, the secrets that lie all about us hidden from our eyes! We glance at a tiny child, and we do not see, we do not know, what a thunderbolt of the Almighty is wrapped up in that little child. 'I walked down the furrow in the field,' said a humble mother who lived on a New Hampshire farm; 'I walked down the furrow with the Governor of New Hampshire in my arms, and the Governor of Massachusetts clinging to my skirts.' She said that afterwards, long afterwards, in her old age. For she knew not then, and no one knew, that her two baby boys would be governors of two New England states" (A. Avery Gates, *Boston Preachers* [New York: Revell, 1927], 212–13).

"helpmate"—a helper with God and with her husband in bringing joy and goodness into a family and into the world.

Women who are unmarried also have a special place as they make a welcoming home and show hospitality to others. Will you thank God for the godly women you know?

LEARNING TO TRUST GOD

✢ Read 2 Chronicles 21:4–6. What is the Bible showing us by telling us that the daughter of Ahab was the wife of Jehoram? What does this tell you about the importance of the role that God gave women?

✢ What is "homemaking"? What are some things that women do to make home a special place? Why is this so important?

✢ *Activity:* Talk about the ways your mother has blessed your family. Thank her and thank God for her. Do something special to honor her this week.

Men and Women in the Church

God has designed different roles for men and women in a family. He has made each husband the head of his home. He has given husbands a special authority and responsibility to lead, protect, and provide for his family. God has designed each wife to help and complement her husband. She is to support and submit to his leadership. They make a great team when they work together as God designed them!

Did you know that the church is like a family? In the Bible those who believe in Jesus and make up the church are called **"the household of God" (Ephesians 2:19).** All who believe in Jesus have the great privilege of having two families: the family that is raising them at home and the family of believers in the church. All believers have been adopted into this family.

Who has headship or authority in the church family? Jesus. Who is its leader? Jesus. He is the head of the church. The Bible says, **"For the husband is the head of the wife even as Christ is the head of the church, his body, and is himself its Savior" (Ephesians 5:23).** Just as there is headship in the home, there is also headship in the church.

As the head of the church, Jesus gave authority to His apostles and prophets. They wrote down His word to the church in the Bible.[1] The Bible is the authoritative word of Jesus to the church. To say it another way, the Bible is in charge in the church. And yet, in the Bible, Jesus instructs the church to have leaders who are in charge of guiding the church to do what the Bible says. These leaders have a type of headship in the church too, as it says in Hebrews 13:17.

Obey your leaders and submit to them, for they are keeping watch over your souls, as those who will have to give an account. Let them do this with joy and not with groaning, for that would be of no advantage to you.

1. See Ephesians 2:20.

So there is a "line of authority" in the church that looks like this:

Christ → apostles and prophets → the Bible → church leaders → all in the church

Sometimes leaders in the church are called overseers, elders, or pastors. This is what Paul says about the type of person an elder or pastor should be:

An overseer must be above reproach, the husband of one wife, sober-minded, self-controlled, respectable, hospitable, able to teach, not a drunkard, not violent but gentle, not quarrelsome, not a lover of money. He must manage his own household well, with all dignity keeping his children submissive, for if someone does not know how to manage his own household, how will he care for God's church? (1 Timothy 3:2–5)

Did you notice Paul says that one who serves as a church leader must be a faithful "husband" and "must manage his own household well"? One who serves as an overseer, elder, or pastor in a church must be a man, because the church is a lot like the family. Just as a man is to be the head of a home, so too are men to be pastors, elders, and leaders in the church.

Women are not to be pastors in the church. This is not how God has designed them. We know this from what Paul says to Timothy.

> Let a woman learn quietly [in the church] with all submissiveness. I do not permit a woman to teach or to exercise authority over a man; rather, she is to remain quiet. For Adam was formed first, then Eve; and Adam was not deceived, but the woman was deceived and became a transgressor. Yet she will be saved through childbearing—if they continue in faith and love and holiness, with self-control. (1 Timothy 2:11–15)

In the church, women are not to be authoritative teachers and leaders. This means that women should not be elders or pastors in the church. Men are designed to lead the church in this way, and Paul points to the story of the creation and the fall as the reason why.

This is not bad news for women. This is good news! As men take the responsibility to give leadership to the church, women are freed up to enjoy all kinds of church ministry just right for them. Women have important jobs. Their work is greatly needed in the church. Women are needed to teach other women the Bible, to encourage and help other women, and to minister to the sick and the poor. Women are needed as children's teachers, missionaries, musicians, and Bible translators. These are only a few of the many things that God wants women to do in the church.

The church is a wonderful family that God provides for believers. Just as following His good design brings happiness to families, it also brings blessing to the church.

LEARNING TO TRUST GOD

✤ Read 1 Timothy 2:8–15 again. What instruction is given to men in this passage? What instruction is given to women? How does this fit with God's design for men and women from the beginning of time?

✤ What ministries are available for men and women in your church? How about for young men and women? Can you do anything right now to serve?

✤ *Activity:* Read a short biography of Amy Carmichael, Elisabeth Elliot, or another woman missionary.

Learning God's Ways

While reading this book about biblical manhood and womanhood, maybe you have wondered, "Why do I have to know this? I am just a kid." Yes, you are young, but you are becoming the man or woman you will be when you grow up. An Olympic swimmer or skater doesn't become a champion in just a year or two. Many start to take lessons and practice when they are children. If you want to be a strong Christian and a godly man or woman, it is wise to start from a young age.

Have you heard of Fanny Crosby? She was a blind songwriter who wrote more than eight thousand hymns. But she started to learn and practice when she was a child. She wrote her first poem when she was only eight years old. By the time she was fifteen, she had memorized most of the New Testament and more than five books of the Old Testament. While she was young, she was becoming the woman who God would use to help other people worship Him through music.

Athletes, like basketball players, swimmers, gymnasts, and skaters, have coaches to help them learn and practice to be good athletes. Musicians and artists have teachers. What do Christians have to help them learn to live godly lives?

Christians have the greatest coach and teacher—God! He is our coach and teacher. His Word is our guide. He has also given us godly people as examples and teachers so that we can follow God's ways. Here is one thing the Bible tells us about that:

Older women likewise are to be reverent in behavior, not slanderers or slaves to much wine. They are to teach what is good, and so train the young women to love their husbands and children, to be self-controlled, pure, working at home, kind, and submissive to their own husbands, that the word of God may not be reviled. (Titus 2:3–5)

How do young women learn to be wives and mothers? How do women learn to care for their families and homes? They learn from older godly women. Older women who love Jesus and have learned to be respectful and kind in how they treat others are examples to younger women and children.

What are the older women to teach the younger women? They are to help them train their hearts to be loving, self-controlled, pure, kind, and submissive or cooperative. How does your mother help you with these things? When you are unkind, she tells you about it and encourages you to be kind. She may discipline you for saying unkind words or treating others unfairly. She speaks kindly and helps others. This is being a good example for you to follow.

Older women should also teach their daughters and other girls how to care for a home. They can show them how to work hard and bring joy to their families. Can you give some examples of this? If you are a girl, do you help your mother do the laundry, fix meals, and shop for the family? How can you make your home beautiful and bring happiness to others?

Boys can learn from their fathers and other godly men. If you are a boy, you can bless your family by helping your father with chores around the house. You can pray for your family and tell them what you are reading in the Bible. You can be a protector, and you can help little children. What are some ways that your father shows you how to be a godly man?

Some boys and girls don't want to work or learn to grow up. They just want to play like Peter Pan did. Peter Pan is a boy in a story who never wanted to grow up. He lived on the island of Neverland with a group of boys just having adventures and never growing up. But this is just a story, not real life. The Bible encourages us to learn and grow in faith and to be responsible—to help at home and work in the church.

When Connor Cress was 15 years old, he read about poor people in other countries. God gave him a tender heart. He wanted to do something to help poor people. So he prayed all summer, and God gave him the idea to make and sell bracelets. Three friends joined Conner. They called their group Dry Tears. Guess how many bracelets they sold? Three thousand five hundred! They also sold water bottles and T-shirts. They made more than twenty thousand dollars. They used the money to dig wells in Africa so that poor people could have water. These boys saved hundreds of lives.[1] They took real responsibility and were not Peter Pans.

You are never too young to take responsibility or to learn about godly manhood and womanhood. You may be just a child, but the Bible says that you should be an example to others as you are growing up. With God's help, you can learn to trust Him and be loving, helpful, and unselfish. Your choices will help you to either follow God's ways or fall into sinful ways. Now is the time to choose to trust God and obey His ways.

Let no one despise you for your youth, but set the believers an example in speech, in conduct, in love, in faith, in purity. (1 Timothy 4:12)

1. Alex Harris and Brett Harris, *Do Hard Things: A Teenage Rebellion Against Low Expectations* (Colorado Springs: Multnomah, 2008), 167–68, 179–81.

LEARNING TO TRUST GOD

✦ Read Titus 2:3–5 again. What do the words "self-controlled," "pure," "working at home," "kind," and "submissive" mean? What are some loving attitudes and actions? Why should you do these things?

✦ Read Psalm 119:9 and explain it. What does it mean to "guard" your way according to God's Word?

✦ *Activity:* Talk with your family about how you can take responsibility or learn to be a godly man or woman. Make some definite steps this week to walk in biblical manhood or womanhood.

Made for Work

Have you ever watched sheepdogs work?[1] Sheepdogs are energetic, strong, smart, and obedient. They are working dogs. They herd sheep and sometimes even cows. They circle around the sheep and keep them moving in the right direction. Sheepdogs can be pets, but they are happiest when they are working. This is because it is their nature to work. It is the way they are designed to be.

Just as sheepdogs are made for work, God designed men for work too. Do you remember what Genesis says about the work God gave to Adam?

The LORD God took the man and put him in the garden of Eden to work it and keep it. (Genesis 2:15)

Eve was not created for work in the same way that Adam was. God made her to be a helper-companion in the work that He gave Adam. Eve was created for Adam, and Adam was created to work.[2]

You have work to do too—like schoolwork. There are books to read and math facts to learn. Spiritual training—growing in faith—is work too. Reading the Bible, answering questions in Sunday school, and praying diligently are good and important work. What other kinds of work do you do? Do you make your bed, take out the garbage, or help in the yard? Are you a volunteer at church? God has made us, and especially men, to be workers. Because God has made men to work hard, there is great satisfaction (a happy feeling) that comes when a hard job is done well.

It is not wrong to play board games or watch a good movie. God has given us times of rest for our good. But it is not good to waste our time when we should be working. A person who is not responsible and doesn't want to work is lazy.

1. If your child has not seen this, you may want to look up a video on the Internet.
2. See 1 Corinthians 11:9.

The Bible calls this person a "sluggard." The Bible has a lot to say about laziness and even gives us an example of hard work to follow.[3]

> Go to the ant, O sluggard;
> consider her ways, and be wise.
> Without having any chief,
> officer, or ruler,
> she prepares her bread in summer
> and gathers her food in harvest. (Proverbs 6:6–8)

The Bible tells lazy people to learn from little tiny ants. Ants are hard workers. Ants don't have a chief or a ruler—or a mother telling them to work hard. They work on their own. No one has to tell them. This is called "taking initiative."

Ants don't make excuses, like "I'm too tired" or "I don't feel like it" or "No one else has to." We shouldn't make these excuses either. When some people in one of Paul's churches didn't want to work, Paul told them to "imitate" or "copy" him in working hard (2 Thessalonians 3:7–9).

3. See Proverbs 12:11; 14:23; 20:13; 28:19; Ecclesiastes 10:18; 2 Thessalonians 3:6–12.

Another person to imitate is S. Truett Cathy. Have you ever eaten at a Chick-fil-A restaurant? Truett Cathy invented the famous Chick-fil-A chicken sandwich. His restaurants earned him billions of dollars. Mr. Cathy also taught Sunday school for more than 55 years. For 40 of those years he taught 13-year-old boys. That is even more important than inventing a famous sandwich and opening more than 1,000 restaurants.

Do you know how Truett Cathy got his start in business? He was only eight years old when he knocked on doors to sell Coca-Cola. Then he sold magazines. And at age 11, he delivered newspapers. Later he and his brother opened a restaurant where he invented his famous sandwich.

Truett Cathy learned to be a hard worker while growing up. His family had a small house with one bathroom. The nine people in his family shared the house with seven or eight others. His mother rented rooms to these people and fed them two meals a day. He helped her with the work. He husked corn, washed dirty dishes, set the table, shopped for groceries, and even cooked. He didn't wait until he was grown up to learn to work hard.[4]

You can learn to be a hard worker too. Don't wait to be told what to do. Start now and find ways to help others. Whatever you do, work hard at it. Boys can show God's good design for men through working hard. What work can you do to bless others?

Whatever you do, work heartily, as for the Lord and not for men. (Colossians 3:23)

4. You may want to read Truett Cathy's interesting autobiography: S. Truett Cathy, *Eat Mor Chikin: Inspire More People* (Decatur, GA.: Looking Glass Books, 2002).

LEARNING TO TRUST GOD

✛ Read Colossians 3:23 again. What does "heartily" mean? How can you glorify God in how you work?

✛ Read 2 Thessalonians 3:6–12. What is Paul saying in verse 11? What is the difference between "busy at work" and "busybodies"? How does idleness (not working) and having too much free time cause problems? How does work help to keep a person out of trouble? (Note: Sometimes sheepdogs cause a lot of damage when they are not given work to do. Work helps them to use up their extra energy. What can we learn from these dogs?)

✛ *Activity:* What work can your family do to bless someone you know? You could rake leaves for an elderly person, babysit the children of a young couple, wash windows in your church, or weed your grandparents' yard. How can you do this "heartily, as for the Lord"? Pray that God will give you the desire to work hard and bless others.

God's Good Design and You

What have you learned in this book? God, the Creator of all things, created us each as male or female. His design is not just *good*; the Bible says it is *very* good. Without God, we cannot understand ourselves or live the best way. We must trust what God, our Designer, tells us.

Do you remember what we learned about God's design for men? God designed men to lead, provide, and protect. He has given them a special job of leading at home and in the church. Men need to be strong, brave, responsible, and self-sacrificing. They need to take initiative and work hard.

Do you remember what we learned about God's design for women? God designed women to encourage, support, and submit to those who God puts in leadership over them. He has given them a special job as a helper and companion. Women must be gentle and cooperative. They need to care for others and for their home.

This is God's design for us, and it is *very* good. It is a perfect design that brings great joy. But not everyone has this joy. Why is that?

Suppose that a master cook made a perfectly seasoned and cooked dinner with all your favorite foods. The meal smells delicious and looks beautiful. Wouldn't it be foolish for you to say, "No, thanks, I would rather have a burnt hot dog on a stale bun"?

It is easy for us to see that this would be very foolish. But this is what we do when we trade God's perfect design for men and women for our own design. God made a perfect, beautiful world and gave man instructions for how to live peacefully here. But man chose sin instead. Man traded God's design for our lives and relationships for his own sinful ideas. Man chose the burnt hot dog instead of the beautiful meal. This is why our world is not full of joy. Sin is ugly, foolish, and selfish, and it brings great sorrow.

Because God is so good, He has given us a second chance. All of us can either love God and follow His ways or can fight against God and choose our own way. This sounds like an easy choice. The problem is that the love of sin is buried so deep in our hearts that we cannot turn away from sin. We cannot love God, His commands, or His design on our own. We need help; we need a Savior. We need Jesus and all that He did for us.

He himself bore our sins in his body on the tree, that we might die to sin and live to righteousness. By his wounds you have been healed. (1 Peter 2:24)

Only by trusting in Jesus can we have a new heart that wants to love God and hate sin. Only Jesus can give us the power to turn away from sin and choose God's ways. Jesus can give men the desire to be godly men, to accept responsibility and lead with kindness. Jesus can give women the desire to be godly women, joyful helpers, and companions. Only Jesus can help them turn away from trying to control things.

Either you are growing into the man or woman God wants you to be, or you are turning away. You are either submitting to God's rule in your life, or trying to be in charge of your own life. You are either believing that God is completely wise in all His ways and that His design is good, or trusting your own ideas.

If you put your trust in Jesus, He will help you to say no to sin and will help you to be the person God wants you to be. It will still be hard at times, but Jesus will help you to fight the battle against sin if you ask Him. Here is a good prayer for you:

Teach me your way, O Lord,
    that I may walk in your truth;
    unite my heart to fear your name. (Psalm 86:11)

In this prayer you are asking God to teach you—to fill your mind with His wisdom and to help you understand His ways. You are asking Him to unite your heart—to take away the love of sin and to give you a love for Him and a fear of rebelling against Him. You are asking God to help you to walk in truth—to obey His commands and follow His ways and design for you.

Most people in the world do not believe in the one true God. They are rebelling against God's good design and will model for you a wrong view of manhood and womanhood. They will do sinful things and will encourage you to fill your mind with their ideas. But if you trust in Jesus, He will be your strength and your wisdom. God has given you a perfect prayer for every day.

Teach me your way, O LORD,
that I may walk in your truth;
unite my heart to fear your name. (Psalm 86:11)

If you do not know Jesus as your Savior, ask Him to save you. Say yes to Him and His ways. Admit that God is the all-wise, good Creator and that His ways are beautiful. Admit that your heart is sinful and that you need help. Jesus will be your Friend, Helper, and Savior if you trust in Him. He says,

I came that they may have life and have it abundantly. (John 10:10)

LEARNING TO TRUST GOD

✢ Read Revelation 3:20. What is Jesus promising in this verse?

✢ Read Titus 3:3–6. How does Paul describe what he and other Christians once were? How does Paul say Christians are *not* saved? How are sinful, rebellious men saved? Why does God save people? Discuss with your family how a person can know whether he is saved.

✢ *Activity:* With your family, make a poster of Psalm 86:11. Put it where it can be a reminder to pray this verse.

children desiring God

This storybook was adapted from Rejoicing in God's Good Design, a junior high Sunday school curriculum published by Children Desiring God (CDG). If you would like to further explore biblical manhood and womanhood or other biblical topics with your child, resources are available from Children Desiring God.

Children Desiring God is a nonprofit ministry that David and Sally Michael helped to establish in the late 1990s. CDG publishes God-centered, Bible-saturated, Christ-exalting resources to help parents and churches train their children spiritually in the hope that the next generation will see and embrace Jesus Christ as the one who saves and satisfies the soul. Resources include curricula for children of nursery age through youth (see sequence chart on following page), parenting booklets, and Bible memory resources. Free parenting and Christian education training audio and video lectures are also available online.

Please contact us if we can partner with you for the joy of the next generation.

childrendesiringGOD.org
info@childrendesiringGOD.org

SUNDAY SCHOOL	
Nursery	**A Sure Foundation** A Philosophy and Curriculum for Ministry to Infants and Toddlers
Preschool	**He Established a Testimony** Old Testament Stories for Young Children
Preschool	**He Has Spoken By His Son** New Testament Stories for Young Children

	SUNDAY SCHOOL	MIDWEEK
K	*Jesus, What a Savior!* A Study for Children on Redemption	*He Has Been Clearly Seen* A Study for Children on Seeing and Delighting in God's Glory
1	*The ABCs of God* A Study for Children on the Greatness and Worth of God	*I Stand in Awe* A Study for Children on the Bible
2	*Faithful to All His Promises* A Study for Children on the Promises of God	(Children Desiring God will announce plans for this title in the future.)
3	*In the Beginning . . . Jesus* A Chronological Study for Children on Redemptive History	*The Way of the Wise* A Study for Children on Wisdom and Foolishness
4	*To Be Like Jesus* A Study for Children on Following Jesus	*I Will Build My Church* A Study for Children on the Church (future release)
5	*How Majestic Is Your Name* A Study for Children on the Names and Character of God	*Fight the Good Fight* A Study for Children on Persevering in Faith
6	*My Purpose Will Stand* A Study for Children on the Providence of God	*Pour Out Your Heart before Him* A Study for Children on Prayer and Praise in the Psalms (future release)
7	*Teach Me Your Way* A Study for Youth on Surrender to Jesus and Submission to His Way	*Abiding in Jesus* A Study for Youth on Trusting Jesus and Encouraging Others
8	*Your Word Is Truth* A Study for Youth on Seeing All of Life through the Truth of Scripture	*Rejoicing in God's Good Design* A Study for Youth on Biblical Manhood and Womanhood
9	(Children Desiring God will announce plans for this title in the future.)	(Children Desiring God will announce plans for this title in the future.)
10	*Open My Eyes* A Study for Youth on Studying the Bible	(Children Desiring God will announce plans for this title in the future.)

Also by Sally Michael

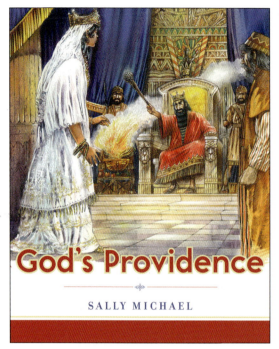

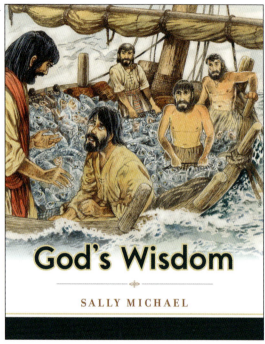

Sally Michael believes that a child who can embrace God's providence can rest in God's sovereign care, and she uses simple truths to help you explain God's providence to all your children. She moves on to show children how God's providence applies to all of life and creation . . . including themselves.

"My heart soars with worship and joy and zeal as I page through Sally's new book, *God's Providence*. . . . Here is a foundation for life that is solid enough to sustain parents and children through the hardest times they will ever face. . . . And here is practical application for children and those who love them enough to teach them."
—JOHN PIPER, Author; Associate Pastor for Preaching and Vision, Chancellor, Bethlehem College and Seminary

Through these teachings and stories from the Bible, Sally Michael describes for parents and children the characteristics of the foolish and the wise, contrasts for them the way of wisdom with the way of foolishness, and shows them the end result of each path. Explore these two paths with your own child, and let the words of Proverbs encourage them on the life-giving path of wisdom.

"Sally Michael seamlessly weaves New Testament and Old Testament stories together to teach biblical wisdom in a way that is clear, fun, and engaging for children. Her compelling word pictures and analogies make difficult concepts easier to grasp."
—MARTY MACHOWSKI, Pastor, Author of *Long Story Short* and *The Gospel Story Bible*